# HOW TO DESIGN GREETING CARDS

BY

ELIZABETH AND CURTISS SPRAGUE

SECOND EDITION

BRIDGMAN PUBLISHERS
PELHAM, NEW YORK

COPYRIGHT
BRIDGMAN PUBLISHERS
JANUARY, 1926

PUBLISHED JANUARY, 1926
ALL RIGHTS RESERVED

SECOND EDITION
JUNE, 1927

*Printed in the
United States of
America*

## Contents

| | |
|---|---|
| Foreword | 7 |
| Christmas Cards | 9 |
|     The Motif | 10 |
|     The Paper | 12 |
|     Composition | 14 |
|     Lettering | 16 |
|     The Dummy | 17 |
| Methods of Reproduction | 18 |
|     Reproducing by Hand | 20 |
|     Linoleum Blocks | 22 |
|     Zinc Etchings | 24 |
| Valentine Greetings | 27 |
| Easter Greetings | 32 |
| Party Invitations | 34 |
| Place Cards | 39 |
| Birthday Greeting Cards | 41 |
| Decorative Covers for Auction Bridge, Score Pads and Tallies | 44 |
| Birth Announcements and Congratulations | 48 |
| Everyday Greetings | 50 |
| Examples of Well Executed Designs | 56 |
| Things to Remember | 61 |

# Foreword

THE custom of sending greeting cards has become so universal that it is to the advantage of everyone to look into the subject and find ways and means of producing original and novel cards by one's own efforts, as this type of greeting is now the most popular and is invariably the one that demands attention and the most favorable comment.

Of the many occasions on which a greeting card is desirable and socially necessary the most important one is that of the Christmas season. In this book we have therefore taken that type of card and given in detail the suggestions pertaining to it. The principles that apply to its design apply equally to other seasonal greetings. With this information concentrated under the one heading and the illustrative plates and analyses following you should not experience any difficulty in designing and reproducing cards for the most unique occasions.

So we will begin with that most general and important occasion for remembering your friends and acquaintances—the Christmas season.

## Christmas Cards

PERHAPS you have been one of the many who experience each Christmas the difficulty of selecting from the cards for sale any which suitably express your personality or conform to your ideas of the greeting you wish to convey. There are always a great many attractive designs, for the Christmas greetings of today have evolved from the lace edged, isinglass, snow incrusted type to reproductions of the work of leading artists of America and Europe, who do not think it beneath their dignity to design and market their ideas to the general public. But the card you buy over the counter, while often well designed and in good taste, cannot be individual. It must appeal to the multitude. Nor does the engraving or stamping of your name in a corresponding type make a card your own. You have probably received many of these "icebergs", all so alike in general appearance that you barely gave them a second glance. The card you received, noticed, displayed and treasured was the one that showed original thought and individuality.

We shall not attempt to show you how to design better cards than you can buy, but we shall try to give you some valuable hints that will help you attain this desirable criterion of individuality if you are interested enough to give the subject a little time and thought.

In treating the subject we are taking for granted that you have a certain ability at drawing, but for those who cannot handle brush or pencil we shall attempt to show several ways in which striking and original effects can be obtained. We cannot tell you how to make your "idea" original. That depends on your own imagination. But we can show you how to develop and reproduce that idea in a distinctive way.

Which brings us to the first and most important part of our subject:

## The Motif

THIS motif may be a purely decorative design made individual by your execution. Or it may be a caricature of yourself or your family, or a photograph of your new baby or your suburban home, mounted in an unusual way. Even the paper on which your design is produced has infinite possibilities. The striking imported papers now obtainable, folded in a novel manner as shown in Plate No. 1, need little decoration to make them stand out from the mass of stationery that overwhelms the mailman during Christmas week. Whatever your idea is it should be consistent with your personality and the part of the country in which you live. If your home is in Southern California it would hardly be appropriate to depict the Christmas spirit of that locality with a snow scene, nor would your garden in Northern New York State be in full bloom during the season you are celebrating. So be sure before you attempt your card that you have a definite idea of the effect you want to produce on its receiver and then exert your efforts to obtaining this effect naturally and convincingly.

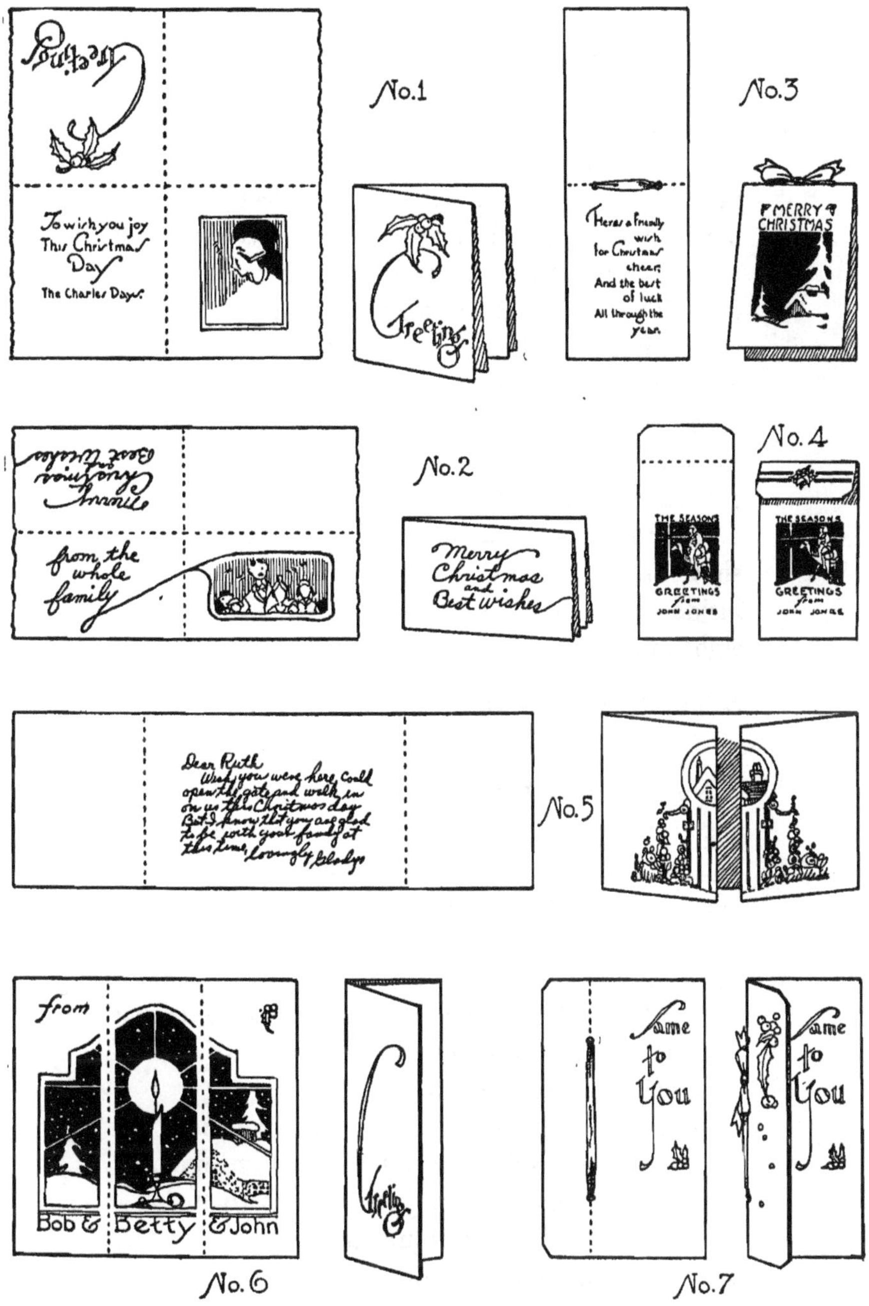
No.1
To wish you joy
This Christmas
Day
The Charles Days
No.2
from the whole family
Merry Christmas and Best wishes
No.3
Here's a friendly wish for Christmas cheer. And the best of luck All through the year.
MERRY CHRISTMAS
No.4
THE SEASONS GREETINGS from JOHN JONES
THE SEASONS GREETINGS from JOHN JONES
Dear Ruth
No.5
from
Bob & Betty & John
No.6
Same to You
Same to You
No.7

Plate No. 1

# The Paper

As touched on above, a distinctive paper folded in an unusual way will greatly enhance your motif. If you visit your stationer or paper dealer you will probably find that he has a large selection of domestic and imported papers in attractive tints and textures, one of which will lend itself to your purpose. The card and envelope should be made of the same paper. If a single heavy weight card or a single fold card is used the envelope should be made from a lighter weight of the same paper. Plate No. 1 shows several ways that light weight paper may be folded to make cards and also several unusual folds for heavy weight cards. Plate No. 2 shows several ways of making envelopes. Both inside dimensions of envelopes should be one-eighth inch larger than the dimensions of the card.

ANALYSIS OF PLATE 1, SUGGESTED FOLDS FOR CARDS

Nos. 1 and 2 show French fold cards. One of the rectangles formed by dotted lines shows size and shape of finished folded card. Fold first on horizontal dotted line away from, fold second from left to right on vertical dotted line. These illustrations also show correct placing of design and lettering before folding. This is an effective way to mount photographs. The use of deckle edge paper is also indicated.

Nos. 3, 4, 5, 6 and 7 show different folds. If heavy card is used it must be scored on opposite side of fold before folding. Scoring is to make a heavy straight line with blunt pointed instrument, so that card will fold on line desired without breaking.

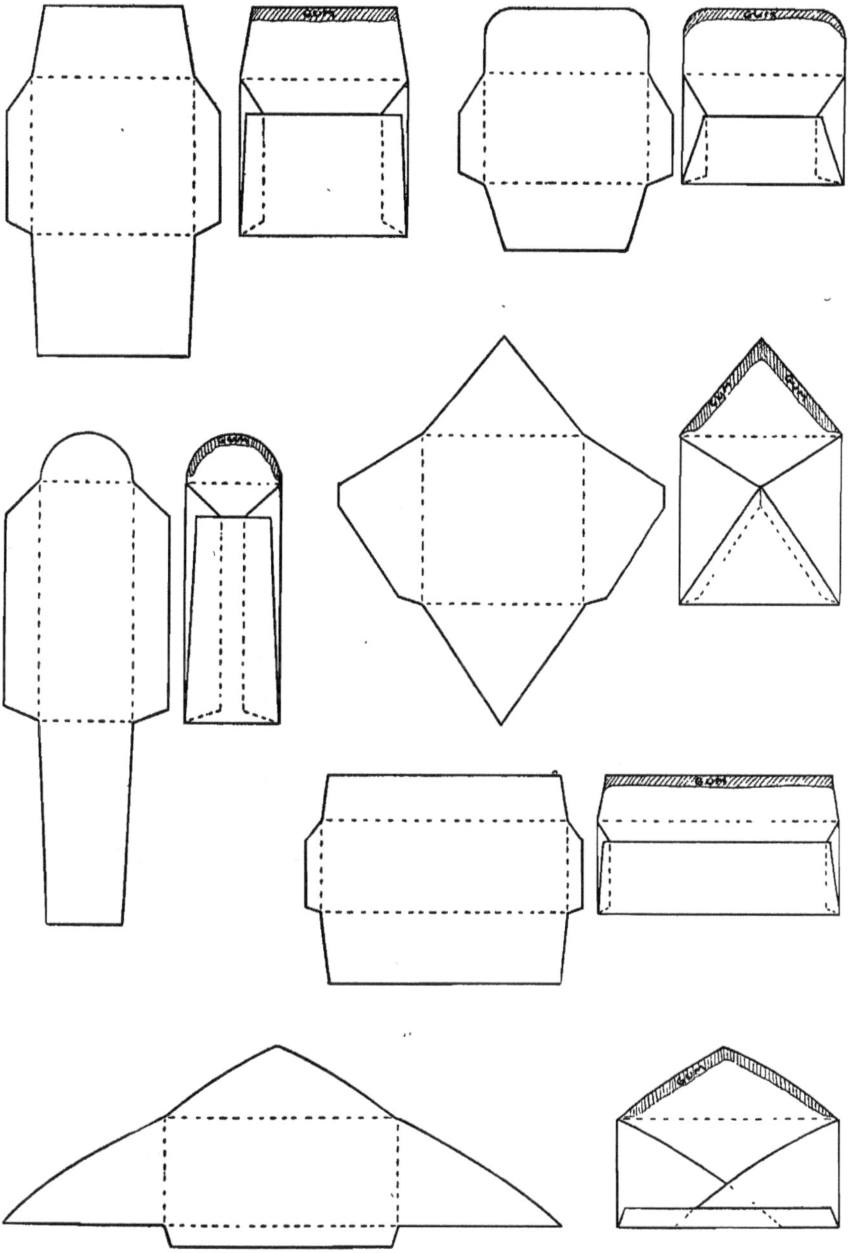
GUM
GUM
GUM
GUM
GUM
GUM
GUM

Plate No. 2

# Composition

IN composing a card you must consider the following: size and shape of card, motif, lettering and color. By color we mean the paper as well as the design. Having decided on the size and shape of the card you will use, in accordance with the foregoing paragraph, it is a good plan to make several rough sketches of your motif, until you come upon one that seems the best arrangement, remembering always that the lettering is just as much a part of the design as the motif. In planning your composition remember your margins. Do not crowd the design or lettering too close to the edge of the paper. Plate No. 3 illustrates how several arrangements of the same idea result in the choice of the best composition.

### ANALYSIS OF PLATE NO. 3

With these four compositions before you the advantage of several sketches of the same motif is clearly seen. Faults become quickly apparent and the best arrangement is easily chosen.

No. 1 is lacking in unity, without sufficient margin and there is lack of interest in the arrangement of its parts.

No. 2 has insufficient margin, the lettering is too heavy and the arrangement is too obviously balanced and uninteresting. Do not divide your card in the middle and absolutely center your motif and expect a good design.

No. 3 could be made a good composition. As it stands it is not correctly balanced and there is insufficient margin. It is never a good plan to divide

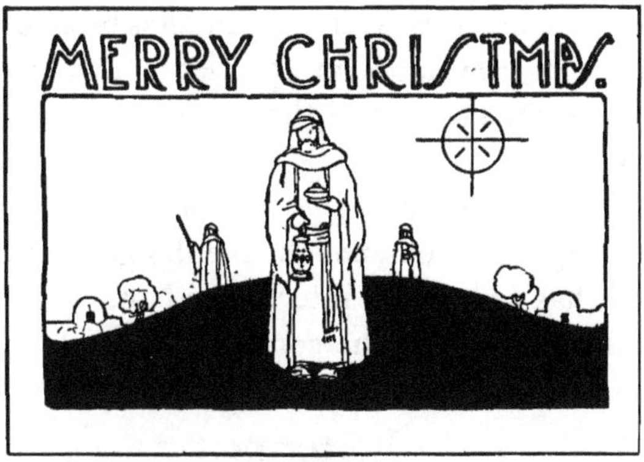
MERRY CHRISTMAS.

No. 1

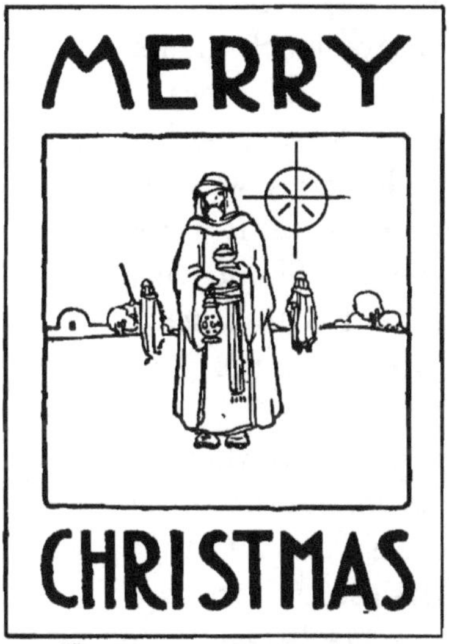
MERRY
CHRISTMAS

No. 2

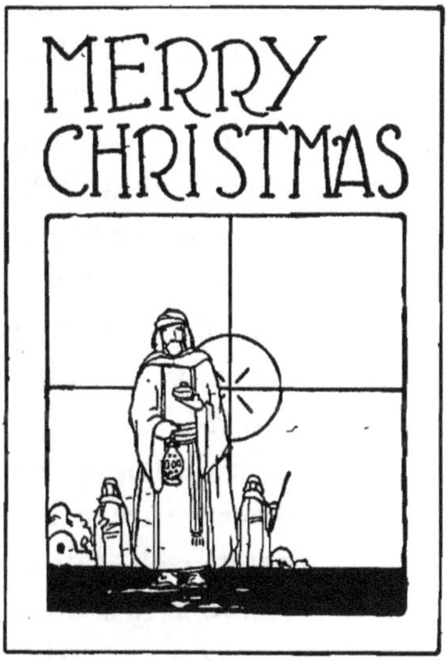
MERRY
CHRISTMAS

No. 3

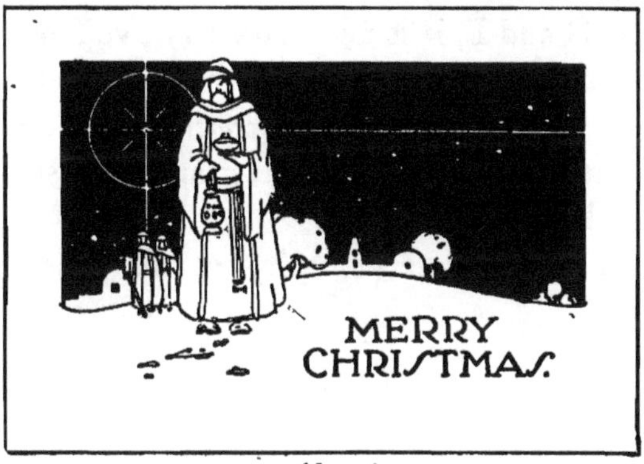
MERRY
CHRISTMAS.

No. 4

PLATE No. 3

a panel evenly as this background has been divided. By placing the figure at the right hand side and changing the position of the star these faults could be overcome.

No. 4 is undoubtedly the best arrangement. The margin is wide enough, the design is well balanced, has unity and interest and the lettering is an essential part of the composition.

## Lettering

WE cannot impress upon you too much the importance of lettering, and it must at all times be considered as a vital part of the whole composition. It must be well designed and in harmony with the character of the motif and sentiment, i.e. it would not be consistent to use Old English Script when you illustrate a humorous incident with a sentiment that reads, "Same to you from the John Browns."

In designing a word or line remember that the space between letters is just as important as the letter itself. For example take the word T O L D. In order to make the space between the letters T and O appear the same as the space between the letters O and L, it is necessary to leave more space between the letters O and L than between T and O. So do not plan your lettering with an equal amount of space for each letter and each space between letters.

You must preserve unity at all times. Each

heavy stroke must be of the same weight throughout and each thin stroke must follow the same principle. If the finish of each stroke or "serif" is large in the first letter it must be similar on all other letters. Also the same characters must be exactly the same in design. An attractive, free feeling may be obtained by staggering the letters of a word, but in so doing remember again that the strokes must be uniform and the design in all letters the same.

The margin for your lettering is just as important as the margin for your illustration. Crowding the letters too close to the edge of the card may spoil the whole composition and result in a cluttered appearance that is most undesirable, as illustrated in Plate No. 3, example No. 2.

## The Dummy

AFTER deciding on the paper and working out the best arrangement of design and lettering it is always well to make a "dummy." That is, to roughly sketch the design in exact size on the paper you are going to use. Then you can fill in the color and see exactly how your finished card will look. With this dummy before you there may become apparent necessary changes in design, lettering or color and these changes can be made before more work is expended on the finished cards.

Analysis of Plate No. 4

No. 1 shows letters spaced mechanically, resulting in a crowded and uneven appearance, owing to the design of the letters themselves.

No. 2 shows properly designed letters. The size of the letters and the spaces between varies.

No. 4 illustrates the unpleasing result of varying the design of the letters.

No. 5 shows the same word properly designed. Note unity of design in character of letters and serifs throughout. No. 3 also illustrates this point.

## Methods of Reproduction

While there are many methods by which Christmas cards may be reproduced some of them are very expensive unless the quantities are large enough to warrant expenditures on plates etc., so we will consider only three inexpensive ways.

If you plan to send only a few greetings it would be too expensive to do otherwise than make each one by hand; or if the subject is such that it can be so handled you can cut a linoleum block from which you can print by hand. If, however, you plan on a large number the most satisfactory way is to have them printed from a zinc etching and then color them by hand. This makes the cards more expensive than the stock cards, but the cost is not excessive and the result may be well worth the additional expense.

CHRISTMAS
*No. 1*

CHRISTMAS
*No. 2*

MERRY
CHRISTMAS
*No. 3*

Greetings
*No. 4*

Greetings
*No. 5*

MERRY
*No. 6*

PLATE NO. 4

# Reproducing by Hand

To draw and color each card by hand is a long and tedious process, but such cards are most attractive and if you do not attempt too many they may not prove unduly burdensome. First trace the outline of your design on a piece of tracing paper and then transfer it to the cards with carbon paper. If the design is to be outlined in black use waterproof India Drawing Ink for this purpose, as it will not run when you put your color in. If you are working on a white card transparent water color paints will be found the most satisfactory. If your card is tinted or colored it will be necessary to use opaque or tempera water color paints, otherwise the tint of the paper will neutralize your color. These paints can be obtained from any art store or can be made by mixing transparent water colors with Chinese White. A delightful effect of a snow storm can be obtained by filling a stiff brush with white paint and drawing your finger or a knife blade across its edge, so that the paint spatters the card. This is illustrated in Example No. 6 on Plate No. 6.

If each card is to be lettered by hand the easiest way to produce lettering is to use the lettering pens. These pens are made with a separate small brass tip which is placed on the pen as a fountain. The fountain is filled from the quill of the drawing ink bottle, just as the ink is put into a ruling pen. As the pens come in about twelve different stroke-widths, it is well to have a pen holder for each size. This will save confusion and time. When the pen is being used it should be held so that both sides of the pen-point rest on the paper. It is not necessary to press the pen for wide parts, as it will almost automatically produce the wide stroke when brought downward and the thin stroke when brought upward.

Some very effective cards may be reproduced by the use of stencils. Designs so reproduced must be very simple, as illustrated on Plate No. 5, examples No. 1 and 2. The lettering on stencilled cards will have to be done by hand as it would be very difficult to cut the characters from a stencil. Remember in designing that you must have a heavy line between each color. This restriction makes them very conventional in character. Transfer the design on to a piece of stencil paper and with a sharp pointed knife cut away such parts of the design as are to be reproduced in color. Press the stencil down firmly on the card so that the color can not run under the edge and then paint the color on fairly dry. That is, have just enough color in your brush so that it will flow. If it is too wet you cannot stop it running under the edge of the stencil and this will prevent your outlines from being clear cut.

Photographs can be mounted very effectively on some of the many folds shown on Plate No. 1. In mounting these use rubber cement, as it will not curl or warp the paper as ordinary paste or glue will do. The sentiment on photographs can be lettered by hand or if you plan to make a quantity you can have a printer set and print it in type. In this case you should make a "dummy" showing where the photograph is to be mounted and where the sentiment is to be printed. Then have the printing done before you mount the photographs or fold the paper.

There are many other ways of making cards effectively, such as cutting out the different parts of the design from colored papers and pasting them to the card: mounting colored illustrations clipped from magazines with amusing and appropriate sentiments for each one; even the illustrations in this booklet will suggest ideas to an original and active brain.

## Linoleum Blocks

Providing the design is kept to simple masses it will not be difficult to cut it in linoleum and this can be printed from a block by hand. Unless you are experienced do not attempt any fine or difficult lines.

Remember that the lettering should be reversed, that is, as it would appear in the looking glass. Cut away those parts of the linoleum which you do not want to print and be sure to remove enough of the fabric so that the paper will not be forced down into the depressions and pick out smudges of ink. Ink the block with printers ink or oil paint thinned out with oil and turpentine, using a small roller to spread it evenly. Do not

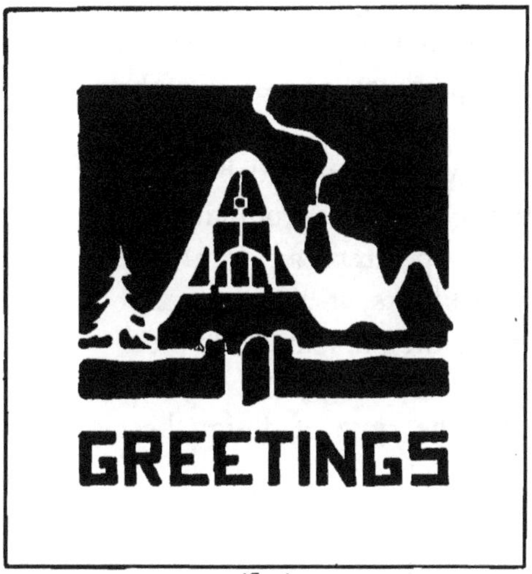
GREETINGS

No.1

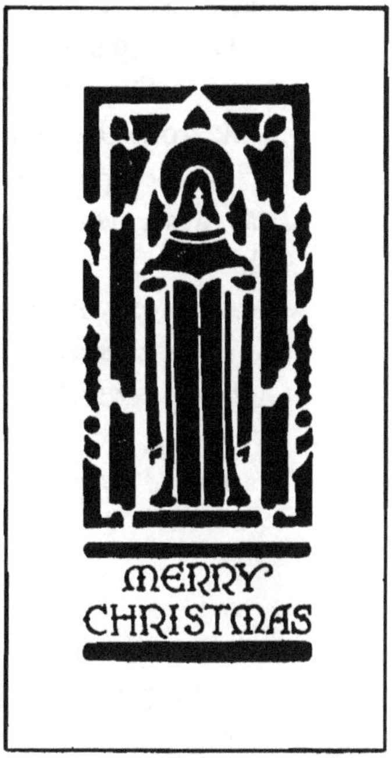
MERRY
CHRISTMAS

No. 2

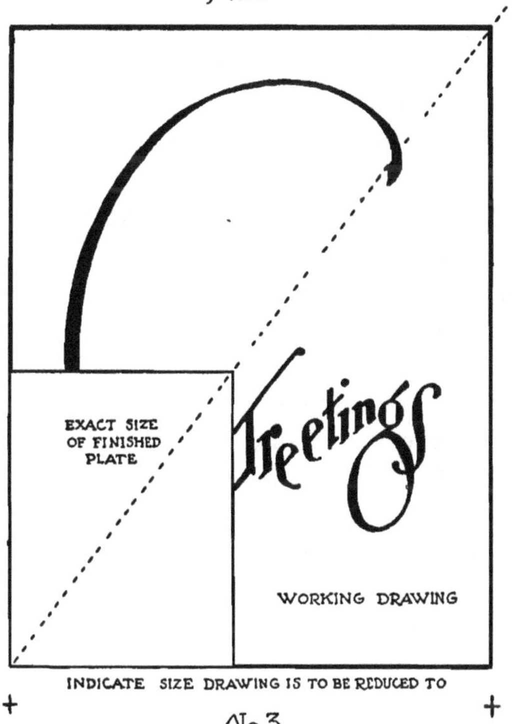
EXACT SIZE
OF FINISHED
PLATE
Greetings
WORKING DRAWING
INDICATE SIZE DRAWING IS TO BE REDUCED TO

No 3

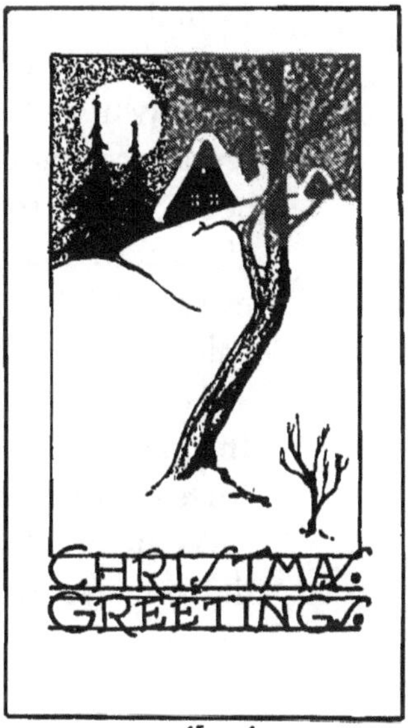
CHRISTMAS
GREETINGS

No. 4

PLATE No. 5

ink too heavily or it will smudge on the edges. Place paper on the block in the position desired and roll with sufficient pressure to remove the ink from the block.

The cards thus printed can be colored by hand as described in the paragraph "Reproducing by hand." If you so wish, a printer can print the cards for you from these blocks, in which case it will be necessary to mount the linoleum on a piece of wood which will raise it type high.

Plate No. 6 illustrates the type of design best adapted to linoleum blocks.

## Zinc Etchings

IN reproducing from zinc etchings the making of the plate and the printing of the card are entirely up to the photo engraver and the printer and all that it is necessary for you to know is how to make a working drawing. Make this drawing on a piece of bristol or illustration board. It must be drawn in India Drawing Ink. A zinc etching reproduces only black lines, masses or dots, so do not attempt to wash in any half tones. It is advisable to make your drawing in line and solid mass only, but it is possible to obtain interesting half tone effects by the use of stippling or spatter. This is illustrated on Plate No. 5, example No. 4. In spatter work you must cut mats to protect the parts of the drawing not so treated.

As it is difficult to execute detail in a small drawing we would advise that you work larger

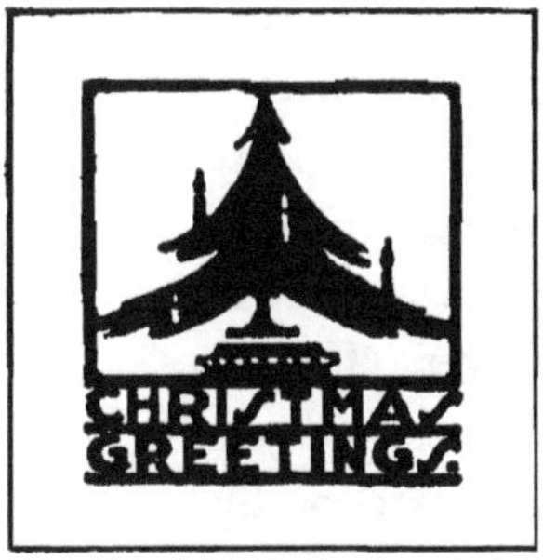
CHRISTMAS
GREETINGS

No. 1

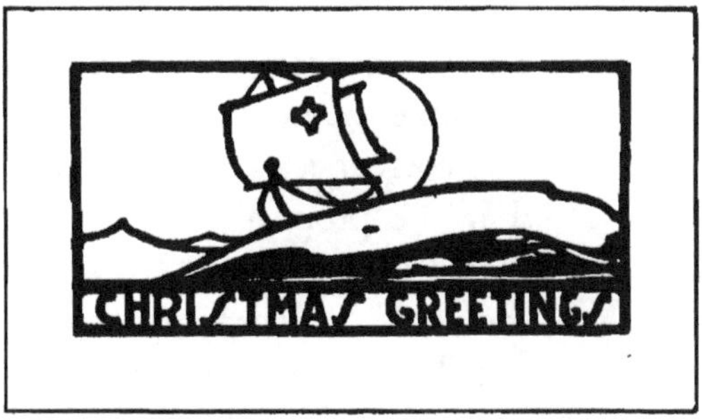
CHRISTMAS GREETINGS

No. 2

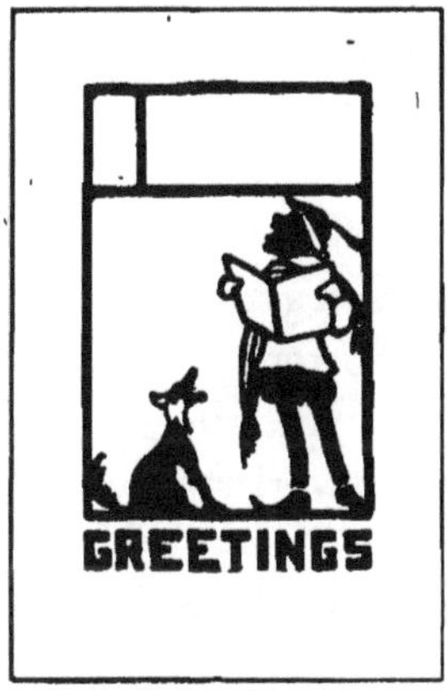
GREETINGS

No. 3

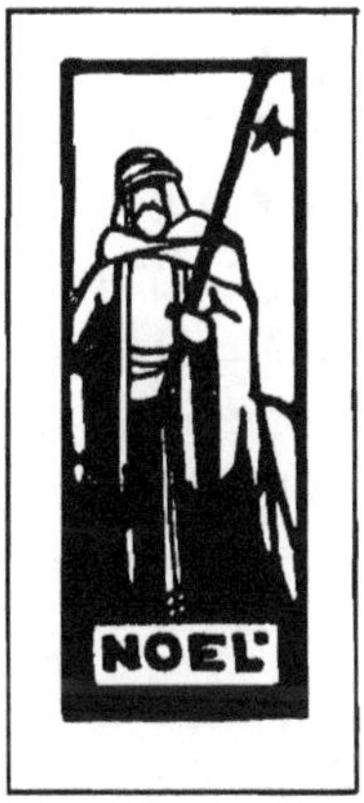
NOEL

No. 4

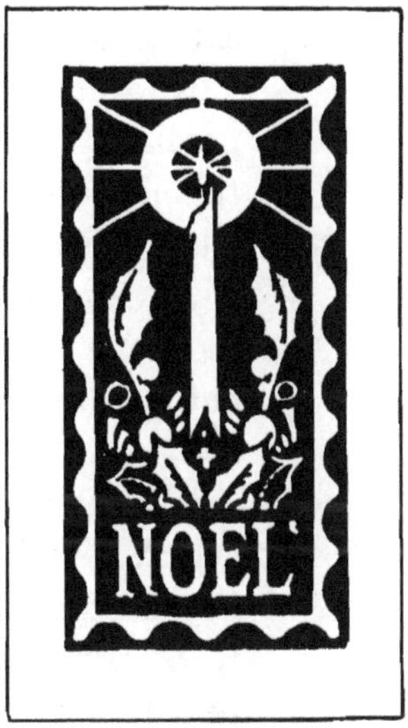
NOEL

No. 5

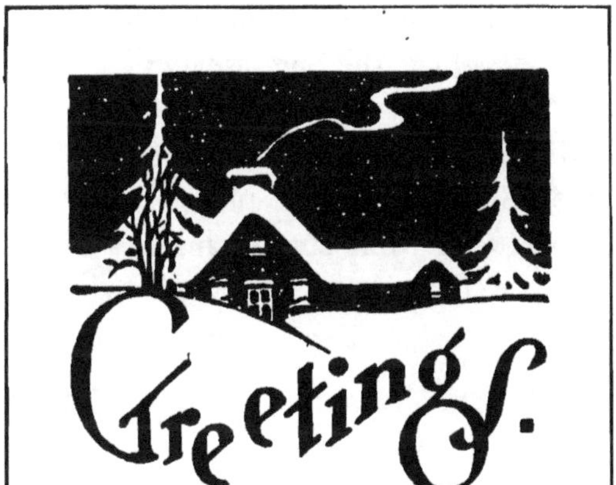
Greetings.

No. 6

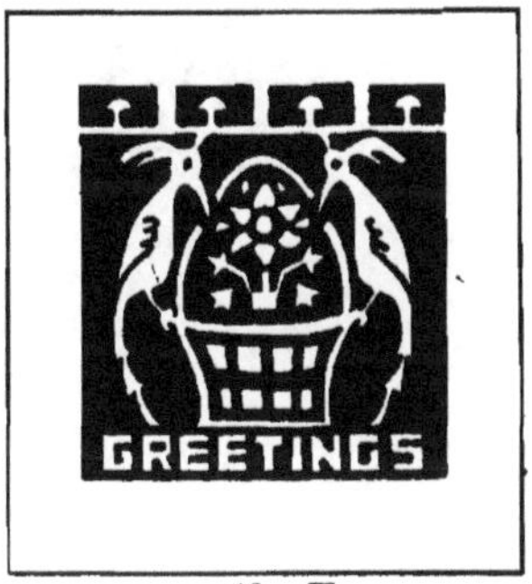
GREETINGS

No. 7

PLATE No. 6

than actual size. You can make your drawing any convenient size, as the engraver will reduce it to the dimensions you desire when he makes the plate. The correct way to determine the working size so that the proportions will be correct is shown on Plate No. 5 example No. 3. In the lower left hand corner of your drawing paper mark out lightly in pencil a rectangle the exact size your card or finished plate is to be. Draw a diagonal from lower left hand corner to upper right hand corner and extend to top of paper as shown by dotted line in illustration. At any height desired draw a line parallel to top of rectangle. From point where this line touches diagonal draw another line parallel to side of rectangle. These two lines together with extensions of the lines forming bottom of rectangle and left side of rectangle will mark the outlines in correct proportion for your working drawing.

When finished, take the drawing to any photo engraver and he will make the plate for you. Before sending the plate and paper on which it is to be printed to the printer, make a dummy in pencil, or paste the proof which the engraver will send you on the paper in the position in which you want it printed. Cards thus printed and then colored by hand are most effective. All the plates in this booklet were reproduced from zinc etchings.

## Valentine Greetings

NEXT in popularity to Christmas cards come Valentine greetings. The motif for a Valentine card or invitation or place card is necessarily limited to the much emphasized heart, but interesting variations are possible with a little thought and inventive genius. Various applications of the heart motif are suggested in the plates treating cards for this occasion and others will suggest themselves if you will concentrate on the subject. The sentiment on a Valentine card can give the whole card dash and spirit if it is original and clever, even though it must treat of the love theme or follow the line of the well known "comics," which we have not taken up here.

## Analysis of Plate No. 7

No. 1 shows a most attractive idea for a Valentine and could also be used for an invitation as well as a greeting. The paper used in this example was bright red on the outside with a white back. The black in the illustration indicates the red side of the paper. It is first cut into the conventional heart shape from a piece of paper about nine inches square. Then, following the proportions indicated on the plate, fold first the sides and then the bottom. The pointed end of the heart will then make the flap of the envelope and should be gummed slightly to hold it in place when closed. The envelope as it appears closed will be about five inches by three and one-half inches, an attractive size for either greeting or invitation. The verse or illustration should be confined to the rectangle indicated in drawing and can be very simple, as the cleverness of the card lies in the unusual application of the heart motif.

Nos. 2 and 3 show the use of playing card motifs to illustrate the Valentine idea. These with other appropriate verses would be especially apt for invitations to a Valentine party where cards were to be the source of entertainment. Place cards, tallies and bridge scores could all be decorated with variations of the same motif and would be a most original way of emphasizing the spirit of the day.

No. 4 is simple in design but can be interestingly varied in wording of the sentiment and illustration.

No. 5 shows a decorative design illustrating quaintly the theme of the greeting itself and could be amusingly colored in bright reds, blues and greens.

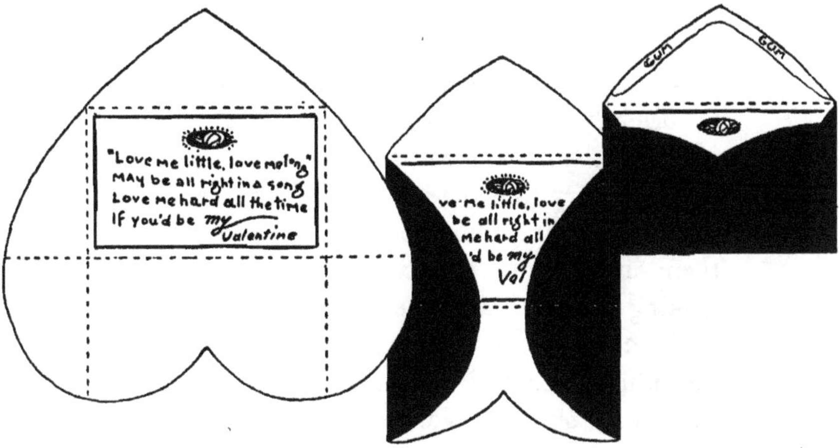
"Love me little, love me long"
May be all right in a song
Love me hard all the time
If you'd be my Valentine
GUM
GUM

No 1

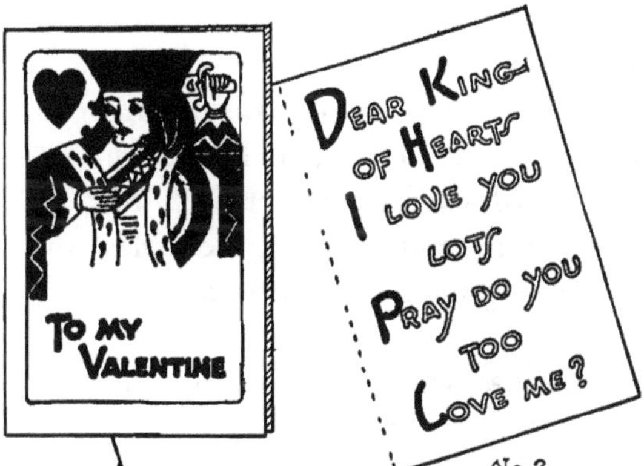
TO MY VALENTINE
DEAR KING OF HEARTS
I LOVE YOU
LOTS
PRAY DO YOU
TOO
LOVE ME?

No. 2

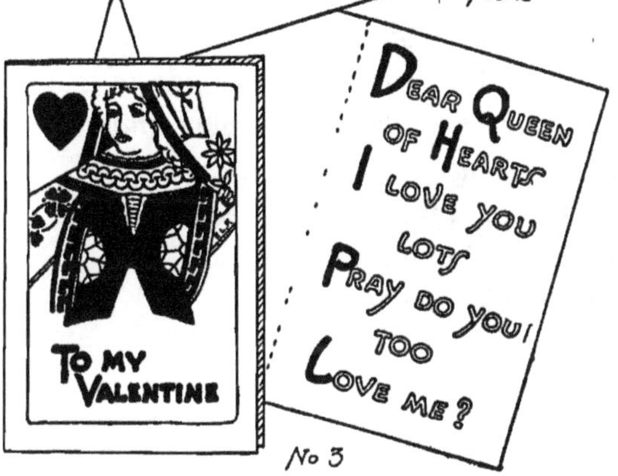
TO MY VALENTINE
DEAR QUEEN OF HEARTS
I LOVE YOU
LOTS
PRAY DO YOU
TOO
LOVE ME?

No 3

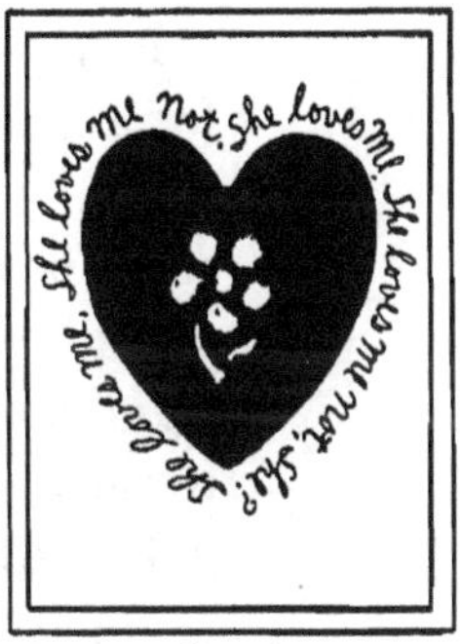
She loves me. She loves me not, She loves me. She loves me not, She?

No 4

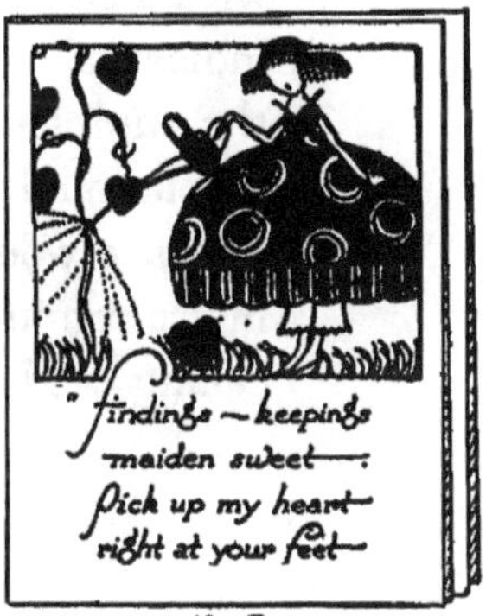
"findings — keepings
maiden sweet:
pick up my heart
right at your feet

No 5

PLATE No. 7

## Analysis of Plate No. 8

No. 1 is an amusing juvenile card and should be brightly colored accordingly. Other verses or phrases in this vein will suggest motifs of design and are very welcome with the children. They can be so simply designed that a child can copy them and color them and have the satisfaction of making his own Valentine greetings.

No. 2 shows how the heart can be folded to contain illustration and verse and this card, together with No. 1 on Plate No. 7 and No. 5 on this plate, should be made of the paper that is red on one side and white on the other, using the white side for the lettering and illustration.

No. 3 and No. 4 show placecards appropriate for a Valentine party.

No. 3 could have an amusing illustration instead of the decorative design indicated. This card should be made of cardboard heavy enough to stand stiffly. First cut out around outline, then fold toward you, after scoring on the back along line indicated.

No. 4 shows an original way of cutting card so that it may be fastened over a glass. This card should also be made of fairly stiff board and cut with a sharp knife around outline and around flap indicated. It will then slip easily over the side of the tumbler. Silhouettes are always popular and can be made very amusing.

No. 5 would make an equally novel greeting or invitation and could also be used as a holder for a calling card if that should be desired.

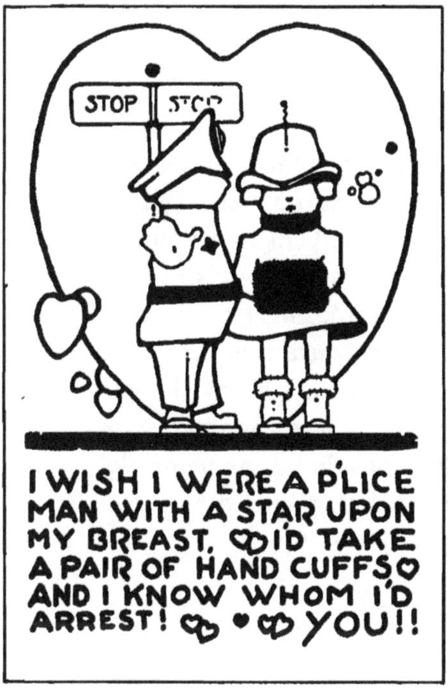
STOP
I WISH I WERE A P'LICE MAN WITH A STAR UPON MY BREAST, I'D TAKE A PAIR OF HAND CUFFS AND I KNOW WHOM I'D ARREST! YOU!!

No 1

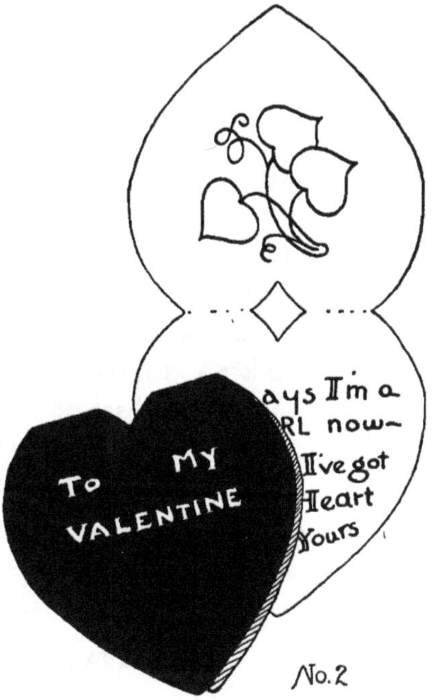
TO MY VALENTINE
ays I'm a
RL now—
I've got
Heart
Yours

No. 2

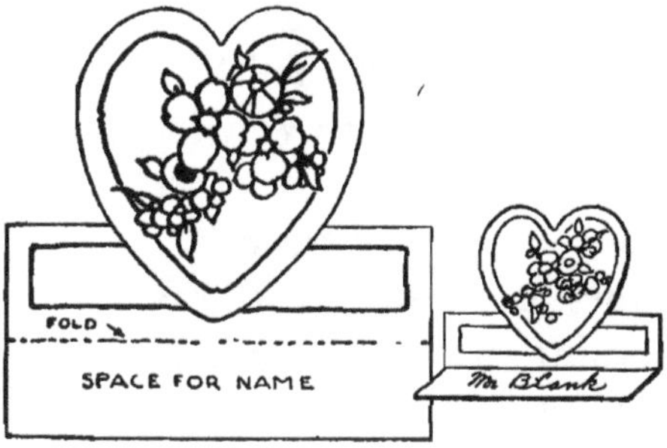
FOLD
SPACE FOR NAME
Mr Blank

No. 3

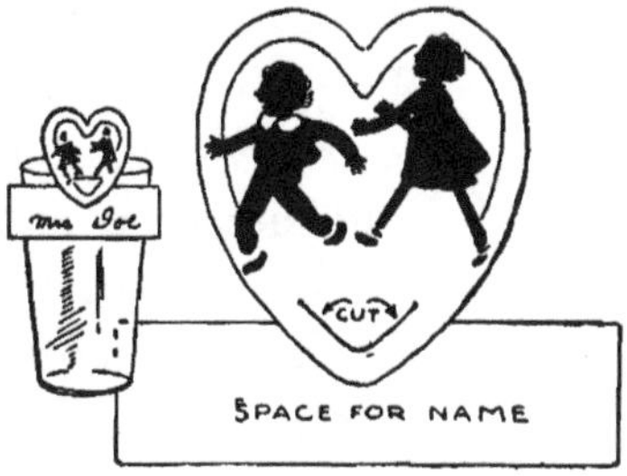
CUT
SPACE FOR NAME

No. 4

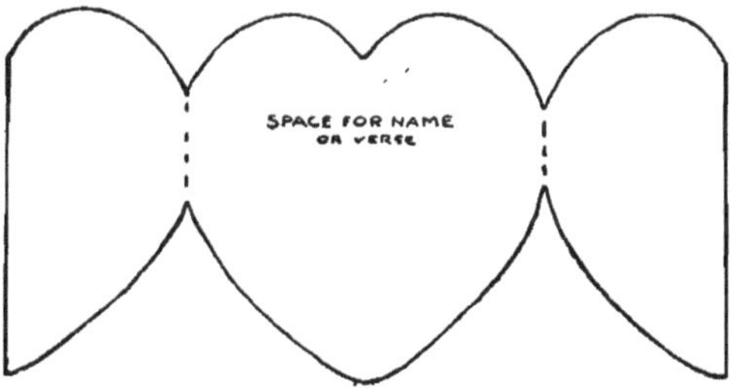
SPACE FOR NAME OR VERSE

No. 5

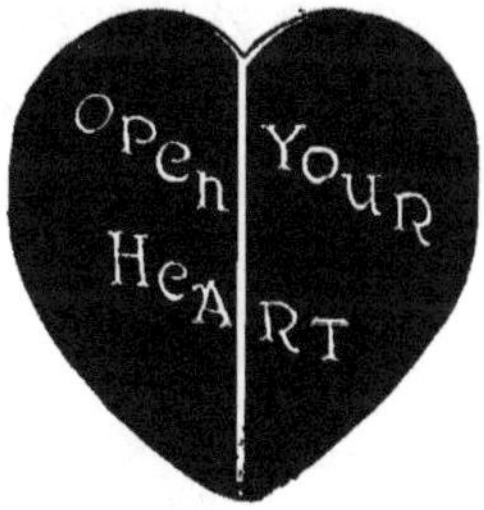
OPEN YOUR HEART

PLATE No. 8

# Easter Greetings

EASTER cards rank next in popularity to Valentines and offer an infinite variety of ideas. Religious designs, floral designs, conventional designs, pretty girl designs—all are permissible and in addition there are the rabbits and chicks associated with the children's celebration of the day. It is particularly important in composing Easter cards to keep in mind the warning concerning harmony of motif and sentiment, as there are many chances to vary both. Even the coloring of your illustration should be carefully considered, as some designs call for a delicate scheme and others can stand a much bolder one.

### ANALYSIS OF PLATE NO. 9

No. 1 shows a religious, kept beautifully simple and free from confusion, with an appropriate quotation to emphasize its message. This card in the original was printed in black on an antique finished, oyster white, deckle edge paper and was left without further attempt at decoration.

No. 2 shows an unusual conventional treatment in the ultra modern manner of a church, with the rising sun of Easter morning in the background and flowers in the foreground. In the original this design was printed in soft gray on a cream colored paper with brilliant colors in the illustration. This design could be cut in a linoleum block.

No. 3 is an application of the pretty girl idea interestingly varied and could be very brilliantly colored.

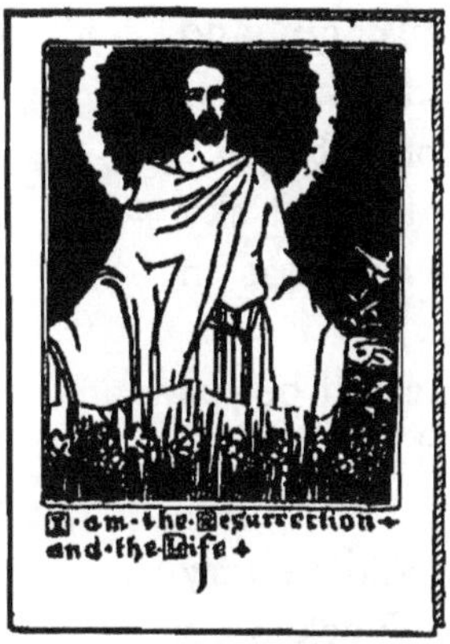
I·am·the·Resurrection·and·the·Life

No. 1

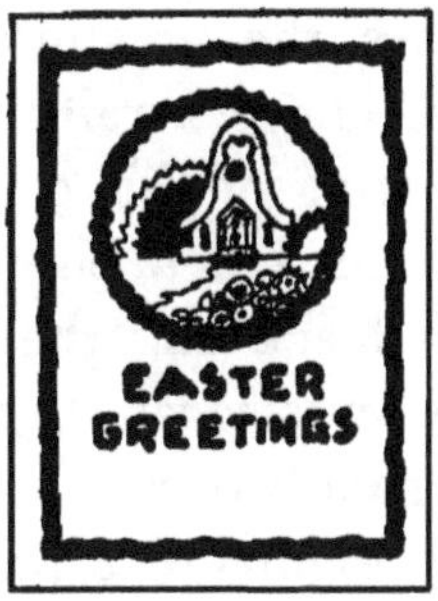
EASTER
GREETINGS

No. 2

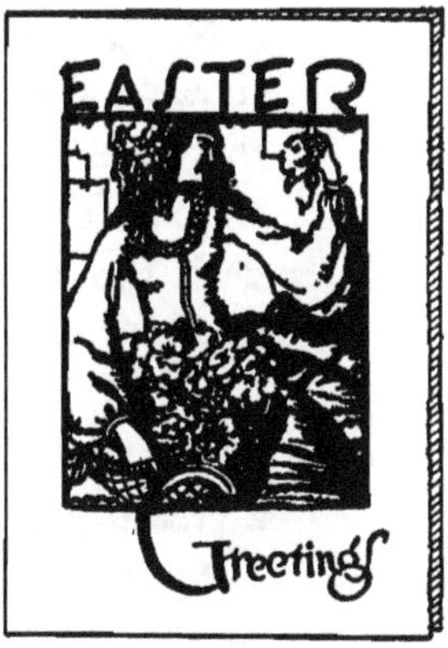
EASTER
Greetings

No. 3

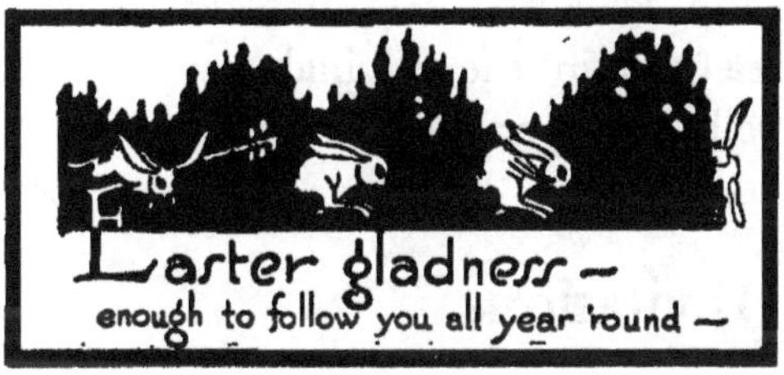
Easter gladness —
enough to follow you all year 'round —

No. 4

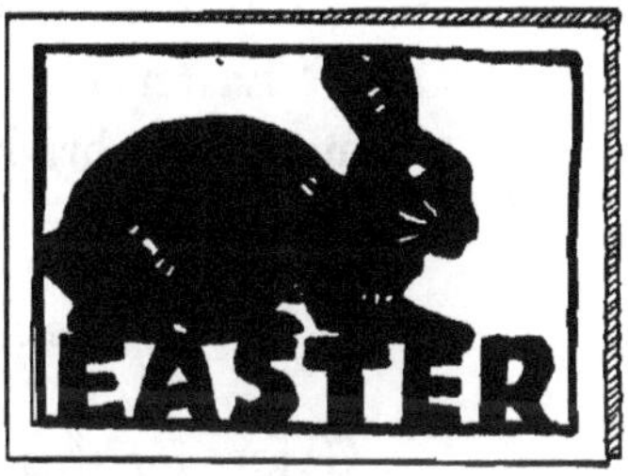
EASTER

No. 5

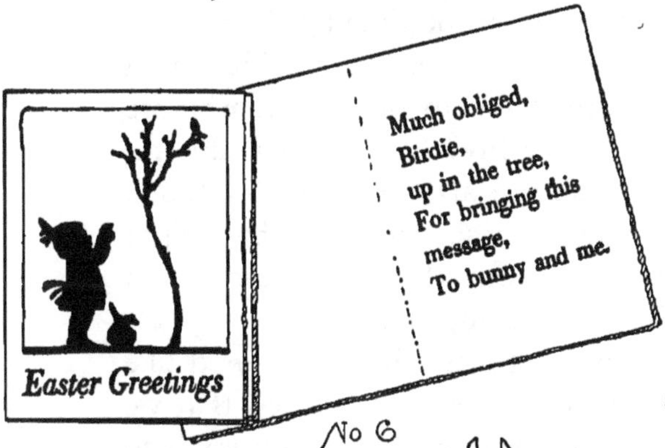
Easter Greetings
Much obliged,
Birdie,
up in the tree,
For bringing this
message,
To bunny and me.

No 6

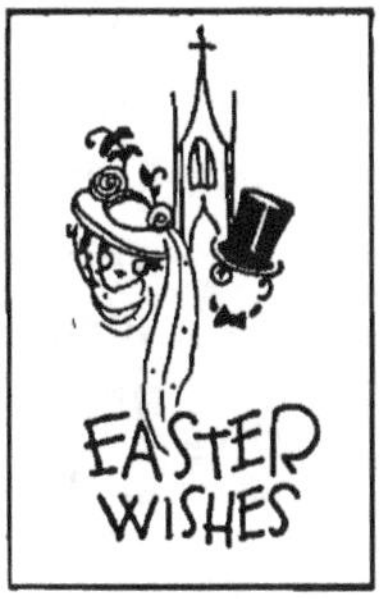
EASTER
WISHES

No. 7

No. 9

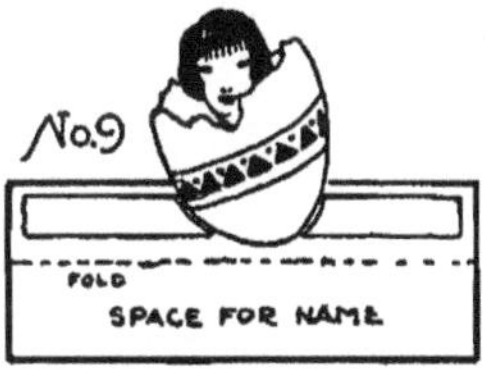
FOLD
SPACE FOR NAME

No. 10

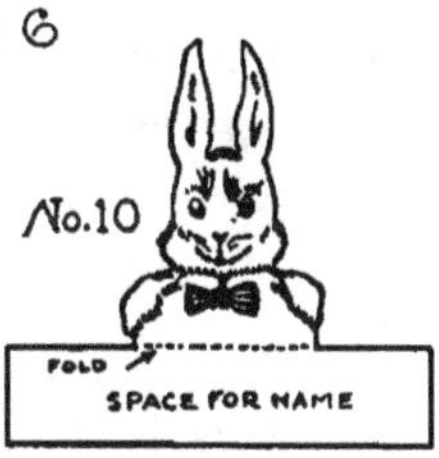
FOLD
SPACE FOR NAME

No. 11

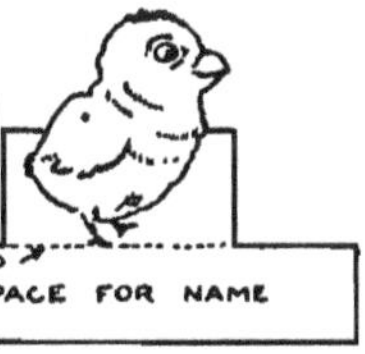
FOLD
SPACE FOR NAME

PLATE No. 9

No. 4 illustrates the greeting amusingly and shows a lighter feeling generally in celebration of the day. The coloring of this card could be very simple. The original had a blue border and sky with the trees in black and the lettering was in bright orange and was most effective.

No. 5 shows a simple design which could be cut in linoleum. The original was printed in gray on a cream paper with no handcoloring.

No. 6 is amusing and quaint and would be very simple to make. The original was in black on a green background, using cream colored deckle edge paper.

No. 7 is a modern and attractive treatment of the "Easter Hat" idea and in the original was printed on bright yellow paper and daringly colored.

## Party Invitations

CARDS for this purpose offer an unusually wide range of possibilities for originality. If the occasion is informal humorous ideas can be illustrated and will cause untold fun to the friends who are the recipients of your invitations. Their zest for the party begins on the arrival of the invitation card and so you must be sure to carry that bright idea of yours throughout the entertainment, so that they will not be disappointed.

There are so many times when one would like to be clever in regard to their invitations that we have chosen as many types of parties as possible to show you how each one may be humorously or decoratively illustrated. Even the more formal occasions, those not formal enough for engraved cards of course, can be charmingly celebrated with simple cards, nicely designed and painstakingly executed, and so much more delightful than a stiff little note or a plain white card with your name and the necessary information.

ANALYSIS OF PLATE No. 10

No. 1 is apparently a most informal invitation and a card of this type would naturally be sent to only intimate friends. A great deal of originality can be incorporated in these most informal of cards and, as we remarked above, one is well paid for the effort by the enjoyment of the recipient.

No. 2 is a more formal type of card and could be sent broadcast among acquaintances. A change of decoration would make it equally appropriate for other occasions.

No. 3 is another type of personal invitation, but not nearly so intimate as No. 1. The name of the host or hostess could easily be incorporated in the design under the lettering or the card might be a folded one and the name inside. This card could be brightly colored.

No. 4 is a children's invitation and could be charmingly colored and executed. Children's parties offer many opportunities for personal invitations for simple verses and quaint designs please them infinitely and are not difficult for one interested in the subject.

No. 5 illustrates an unusually charming card celebrating a house warming. Can you not imagine that a person receiving this card would make every effort to attend the party, and would be sure that any friends of such a charming couple would be well worth meeting? Such ideas need expression and are always appreciated.

No. 6 shows a tiny card that a young matron might execute in spare moments. It is decidedly informal and we would judge that these friends of hers are all quite intimate ones, but that she took this original way of bidding them to her luncheon rather than using the prosaic telephone. The anticipation of her guests would be greatly enhanced by her clever card of invitation.

No. 7 shows a more formal card that might be either lettered by hand or engraved. It is restrained and in perfectly good taste, yet is a welcome departure from the stiffly formal cards that have prevailed in the past.

No. 8 is another very personal invitation with plenty of pep and punch, as is fitting for the occasion it bids you celebrate. A red, white and blue color scheme could do much in helping carry out the clever idea.

No. 9 is even more personal and a card of this type could be made tremendously amusing. Any personal touch that contributes to the fun is perfectly permissible in a card like this, however ridiculous it may be. If you can get any suggestion of likeness or caricature the persons represented you will find yourself congratulated on your cleverness.

### No 1
YOU MUST COME OVER
New Years Eve at our
from 'till you are
ready to go home-
**HAPPY NEW YEAR**
THE JACK BROWNS

### No 2
You are cordially
invited to attend
a Colonial Ball
at Meredith College
on
Washington's Birthday

### No. 3
A Jack O-Lantern and
a ghost
Will be at our front door
To welcome you on
Hallowe'en
There's lots of fun in store

### No. 4
I'm giving a
Masquerade
Party
October tenth
is the date
The Grand March
starts at Carrington
Hall
Sharp on the stroke
of eight
MARY DOE

### No. 5
We've moved into
our brand new house
It's small but quite complete,
And we want you there
on Thursday night
Our other friends to meet
CLARA AND CHARLES WHITE

### No 6
A luncheon I'm giving at my house
For you and some other dames
On Tuesday next at two o'clock
Can you make it?
(SIGNED) Mary James

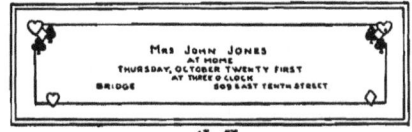

### No. 7
MRS JOHN JONES
AT HOME
THURSDAY, OCTOBER TWENTY FIRST
AT THREE O'CLOCK
BRIDGE    505 EAST TENTH STREET

### No. 8
Just show your independence
And come around at eight
We'll eat and pop pop-crackers
And then we'll celebrate
B.Y.O.L.
JULY 4th
TED SMITH

### No. 9
On April eleventh me and my mate
Will have lived together for ten
years straight
We feel that's a lot to celebrate
So join the party and don't be late
THE JOHN BLANKS

PLATE No. 10

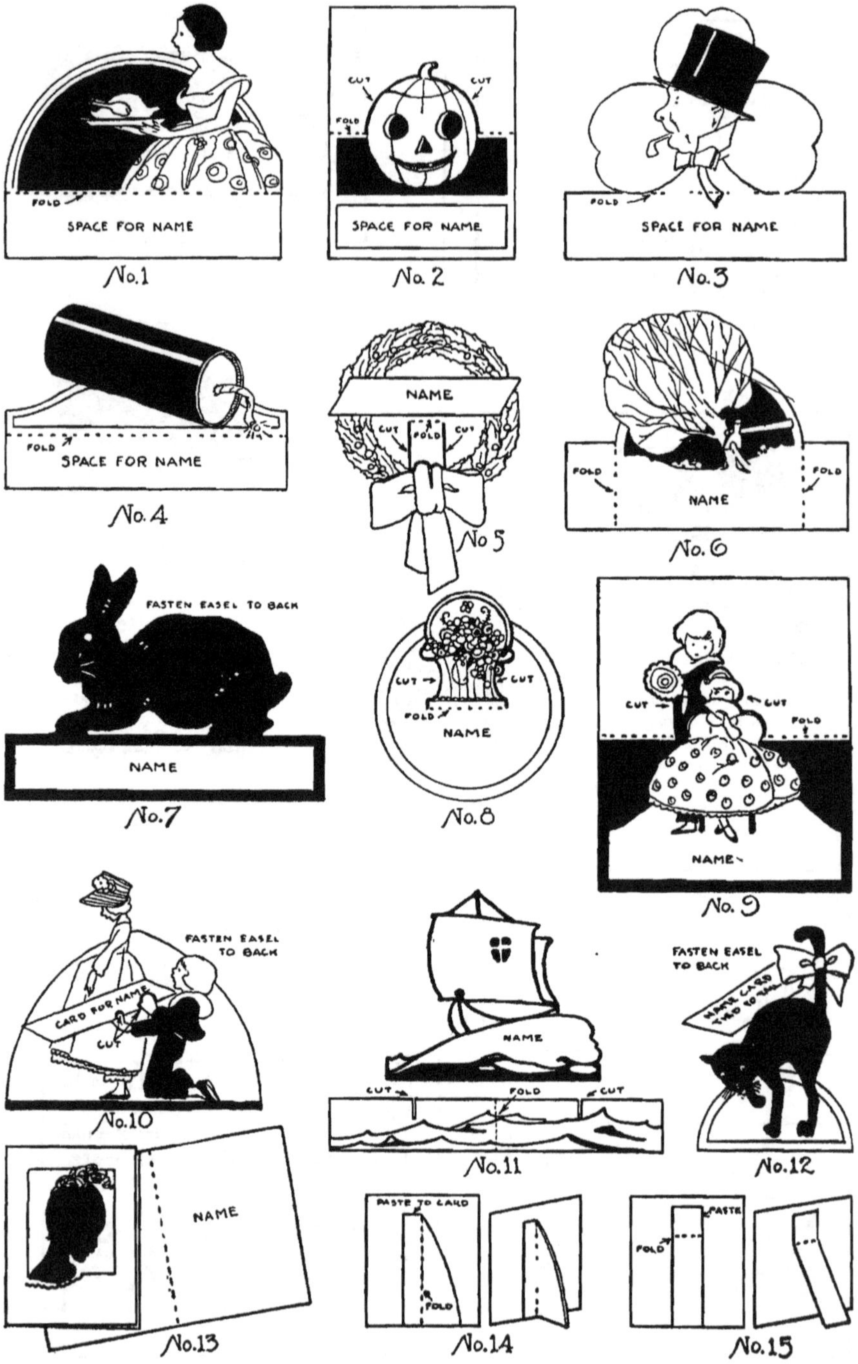

FOLD
SPACE FOR NAME
No. 1
CUT
CUT
FOLD
SPACE FOR NAME
No. 2
FOLD
SPACE FOR NAME
No. 3
FOLD
SPACE FOR NAME
No. 4
NAME
CUT
FOLD
CUT
No. 5
FOLD
FOLD
NAME
No. 6
FASTEN EASEL TO BACK
NAME
No. 7
CUT
CUT
FOLD
NAME
No. 8
CUT
CUT
FOLD
NAME
No. 9
FASTEN EASEL TO BACK
CARD FOR NAME
CUT
No. 10
NAME
CUT
FOLD
CUT
No. 11
FASTEN EASEL TO BACK
NAME CARD TIED TO TAIL
No. 12
NAME
No. 13
PASTE TO CARD
FOLD
No. 14
PASTE
FOLD
No. 15


PLATE No. 11

# Place Cards

AFTER party invitations our mind naturally proceeds to further embellishment of the party itself and place cards appear necessary. Plate No. 11 gives you some idea of the large variety of types that are possible and there are many more we haven't the space to show. A great many of the place cards illustrated are of the cut out kind, which, while not necessary, gives an opportunity for interest greater than a plain card. Attractive cut outs other than the ones illustrated may come to you. All place cards should be made of kid finished bristol board in a weight heavy enough to support the cut out, if that type of card is used. These bristols come in tints that might blend with your design and you would do well to investigate these colors before buying the plain white.

### ANALYSIS OF PLATE No. 11

No. 1 is a Thanksgiving card admirably illustrating the spirit of that day. After the design is drawn on the card the outline should be cut out with a sharp knife and the card scored on the back and folded as indicated in the illustration.

No. 2, a Hallowe'en card, is so designed that it makes its own easel, after being cut on lines indicated and folded as instructed above. This card would naturally be colored bright orange and black.

No. 3 for St. Patrick's Day would be made along the same method and emerald green used for the coloring.

No. 4 is simple in design and easy of execution and would be bright and gay with its flaming red pop cracker.

No. 5 illustrates another card designed to go over a tumbler. The holly wreath in green and red with a red ribbon would be most decorative for a Christmas dinner. Care should be taken in cutting a card of this kind as a slip of the knife might ruin your work.

No. 6 for Washington's Birthday is another card that makes its own easel and carries out the traditions of the day.

No. 7 shows how a motif used for an Easter card can be adapted to other purposes. This could be brightly colored and by fastening the easel to the back you would have an attractive place card for an Easter dinner party.

No. 8 is purely decorative in design and could be colored to harmonize with any flower scheme you might be using. The cut out in this card would stand erect, using the circular name plate for its base.

No. 9 illustrates the use of figures in cut out place cards. By cutting around the upper part of these as indicated and folding back the body of the card you have an attractive cut out that can be varied for many different types.

No. 10 shows another attractive way of inserting the name card. By cutting out the boy's hands the card can be inserted in the slits and removed easily. This card will need an easel attached to the back.

No. 11 is an unusually attractive idea and would be peculiarly apt for a "Bon Voyage" or farewell party given for a friend. The stand representing the ocean is folded in the middle after being slit to hold the ship and then the cut out is inserted.

No. 12 is another idea for a Hallowe'en party and in this drawing is shown the black cat traditional to that day. With a yellow or orange ribbon a plain white name card is tied to his tail and an easel attached to the back of the card holds it erect.

No. 13 would be charming for a girl's party. The silhouettes could be varied infinitely. The name might be put on the cover and an amusing personal verse or humorous phrase inserted inside the card.

No. 14 and No. 15 show two types of easels that could be easily cut out and attached to those cards needing this method of support.

## Birthday Greeting Cards

WHILE birthdays come but once a year, they are of tremendous importance to us all and a card showing your remembrance of that day will delight the youngster and flatter the oldsters who are rather inclined to slur the date and pass it by. We have shown both decorative and humorous ideas in the plate treating this subject and many more ideas are possible on the theme. Even though you are sending a gift in addition to the card a bit of humor or sentiment is never amiss and can be slipped in with the package to cause delight and smiles to its recipient.

## Analysis of Plate No. 12

No. 1 shows a charming silhouette that can be left in black and white or brightened with a bit of color in the flowers and veil. All silhouetes stand out best on a plain white card, as was used in the original of this illustration. The sentiment is appropriate and simple and should give an idea of composing more personal ones for special friends.

No. 2 admirably illustrates an informal greeting that is at the same time cordial and clever. It is simple in design and execution and a bit of color could be introduced, as in the original by printing the first letter of the greeting and the whole last line in red. No other attempt at color will be necessary.

No. 3 is charmingly youthful and while used as a greeting could be very easily adapted as an invitation. The original was printed on a buff colored card, the background green with touches of the same color in the girl's dress and the figures were in black and yellow. It would be most attractive for a children's invitation.

No. 4 and No. 5 show further silhouettes which are simple in design yet have a peculiar charm of their own.

No. 6 and No. 7 illustrate the humorous type of birthday that is so often desirable. Many clever phrases and verses are possible along these lines and ridiculous illustrations will add to their hilarity.

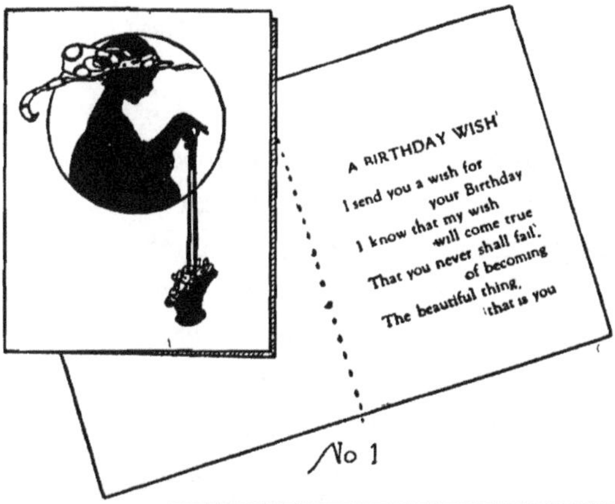
A BIRTHDAY WISH
I send you a wish for
your Birthday
I know that my wish
will come true
That you never shall fail,
of becoming
The beautiful thing,
that is you

No 1

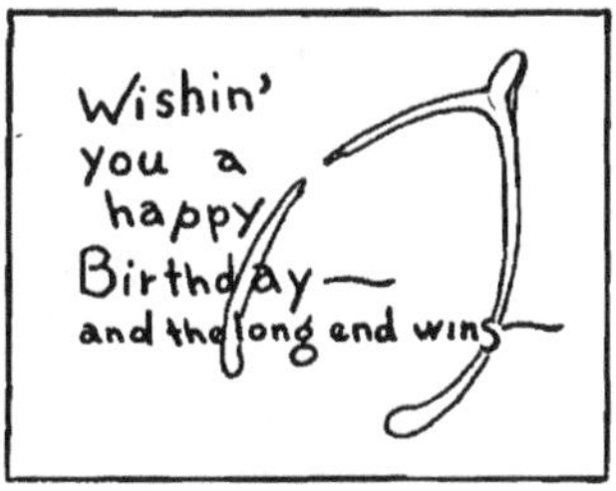
Wishin'
you a
happy
Birthday—
and the long end wins—

No. 2

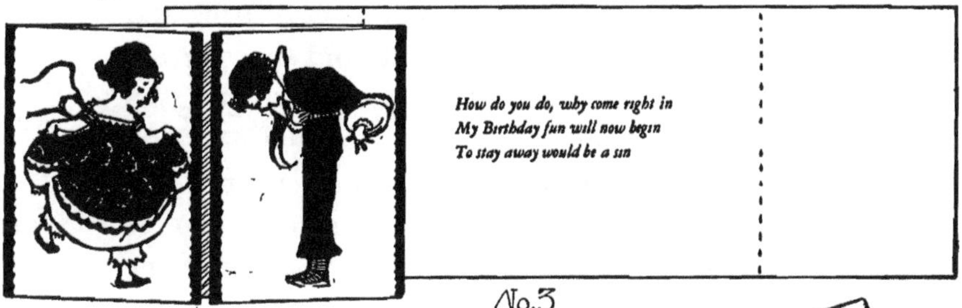
How do you do, why come right in
My Birthday fun will now begin
To stay away would be a sin

No. 3

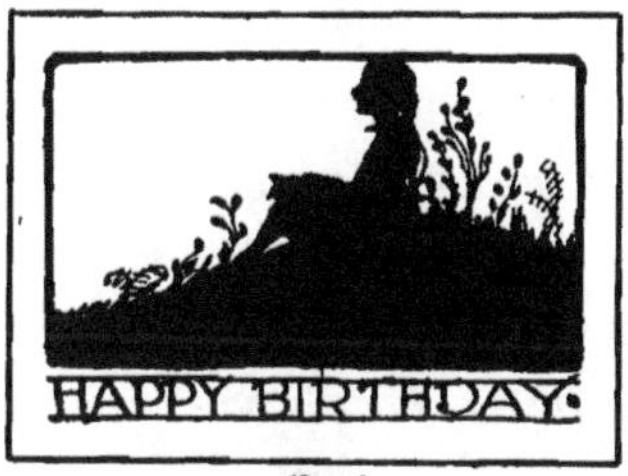
HAPPY BIRTHDAY

No. 4

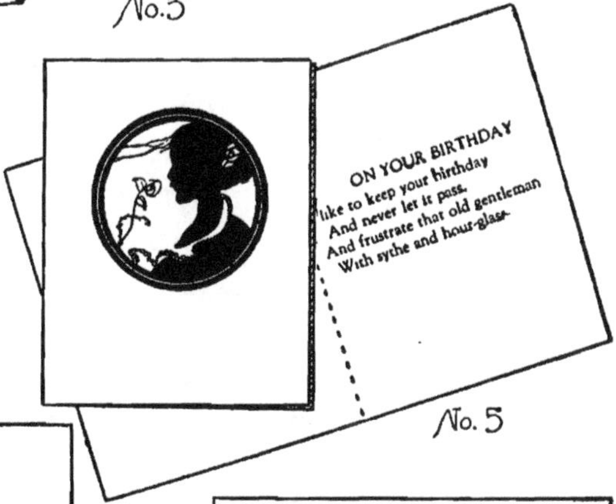
ON YOUR BIRTHDAY
like to keep your birthday
And never let it pass,
And frustrate that old gentleman
With sythe and hour-glass

No. 5

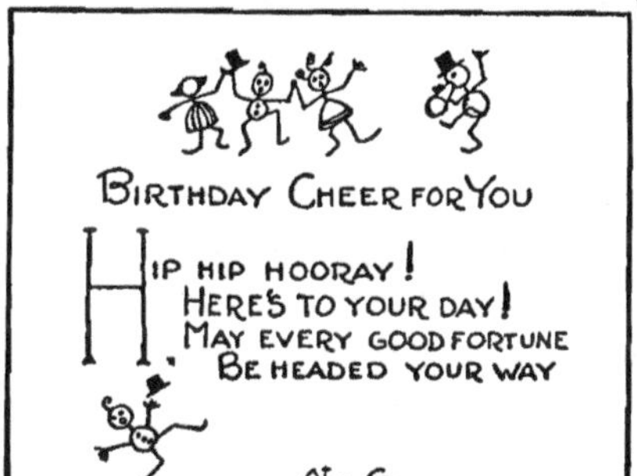
BIRTHDAY CHEER FOR YOU
HIP HIP HOORAY!
HERE'S TO YOUR DAY!
MAY EVERY GOOD FORTUNE
BE HEADED YOUR WAY

No. 6

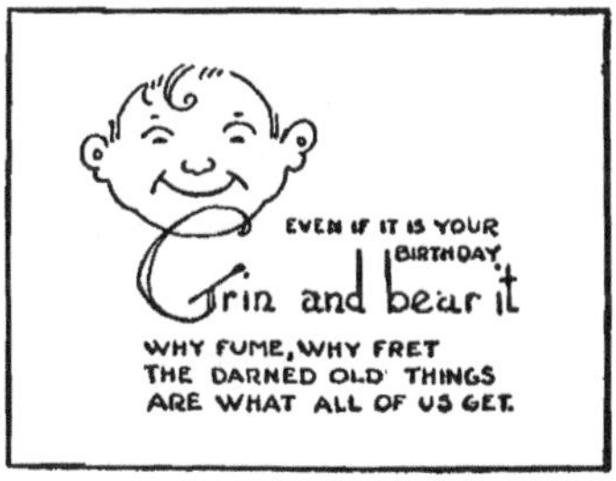
EVEN IF IT IS YOUR
BIRTHDAY
Grin and bear it
WHY FUME, WHY FRET
THE DARNED OLD THINGS
ARE WHAT ALL OF US GET.

No. 7

PLATE NO. 12

# Decorative Covers For Auction Bridge Score Pads and Tallies

THE enormous popularity of Auction Bridge leads us to include in this book on "Greeting Cards" a page of suggestions that can be variously adapted for your uses. If one is sufficiently energetic it would be delightful to make these accessories for one's own use, but our idea in incorporating these suggestions with our other instructions was a different one. What could be more charming for a gift or a bridge prize than a set of pads and tallies, attractively hand colored and showing the individuality and taste of the giver as no gift purchased in the shops could do? It would not be a difficult feat and would give great satisfaction, we are sure. Almost any decorative subject can be used as a motif on bridge pad covers, and if the tallies are to be included in the set, simpler designs on the same paper, of the same motif should be used. You can purchase at any stationery store the necessary pads and attractive papers in which they can be covered. Your next problem will be to decide the best method of covering the plain pad. Both bottom and side openings are used, though the side opening seems the more popular. In planning the size of your cover there are a few things to be considered. To make a finished product the cover should be of one piece and make a front and back cover. In cutting the paper you must allow at least one-eighth inch margin on all sides and on the side which will fold around the pad you must allow the extra thickness of the pad. It is more convenient to lay out on this flat paper the position of your design and execute it fully before pasting in the pad. After the design is fully finished lay it face down on the table and, taking up your pad, put paste on its cardboard back, as close to its binding as possible, and on a small area. Do not cover the whole back of the pad with paste as that will probably draw it and make it warp as it dries. Then allowing for the margins you have planned in cutting your paper place the pad on the paper and put under a weight until it dries.

Tallies are usually about two and one-quarter inches by five and three-quarter inches, but this size can be varied interestingly according to your own ingenuity. If tassels are not available ribbon ties are very pretty.

## Analysis of Plate No. 13

No. 1 illustrates a set of four table number score pads and four designs for the necessary sixteen tallies to complete the set. This set is a very good example of several points that should be kept in mind in designing pads and tallies. First, the composition has been admirably adapted to the shape of the score pad. Second, the table numbers have the necessary prominence. These should always be strong, not only in position and size but also in color, as they are in a case of this kind the most important part of the composition. Third, the decorative motif of the pads is carried consistently through the designs on the tallies. The accepted method of ruling the back of the tallies is also illustrated though this is not absolutely necessary.

No. 2 illustrates an attractive idea of monogramming bridge pads. A few of these would make a most acceptable gift and would be charmingly individual for one's own use. The background illustrated was obtained in the following manner: a mat was cut to protect the white border and the oval for the monogram and fastened in place with rubber cement. A stencil was placed over the cover, fastened down securely with rubber cement and the cover was then spattered with color. We recommend the use of rubber cement as it will hold fast and yet on the removal of parts will clean off easily and leave the paper unmarked.

No. 3 and No. 4 illustrate pads open at the bottom end and also how different types of motif are applicable to bridge score covers.

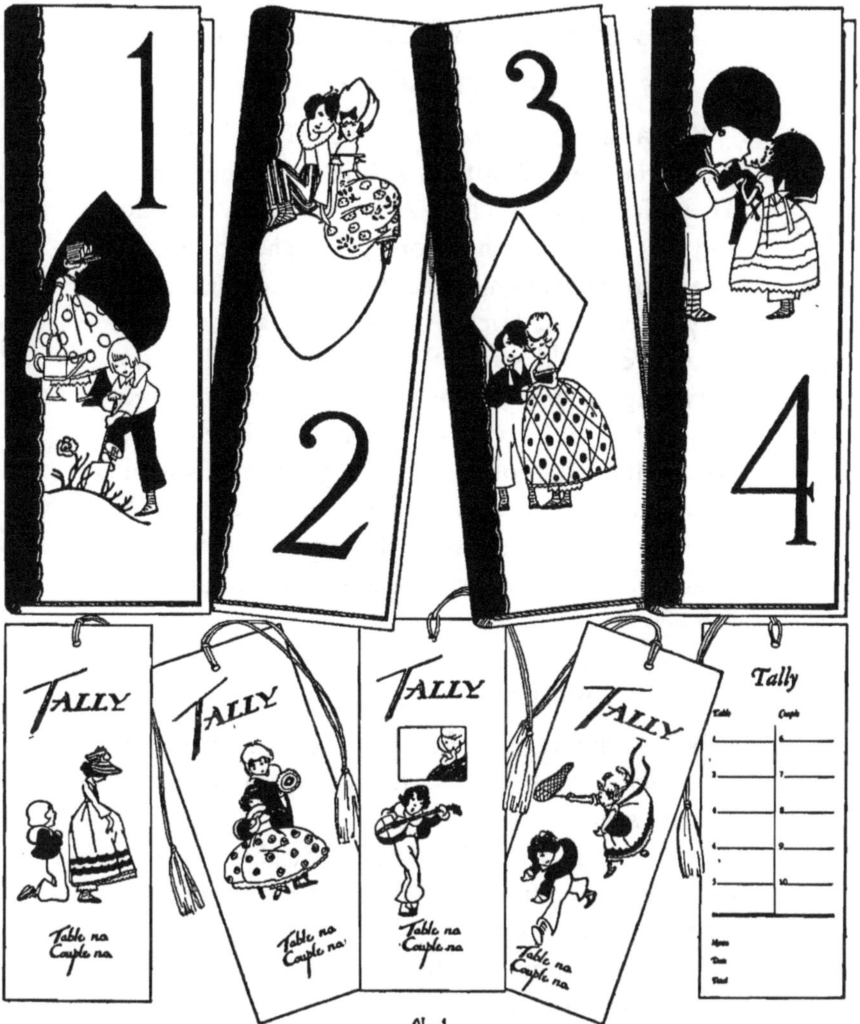
1
2
3
4
TALLY
Table no
Couple no
Tally
No 1

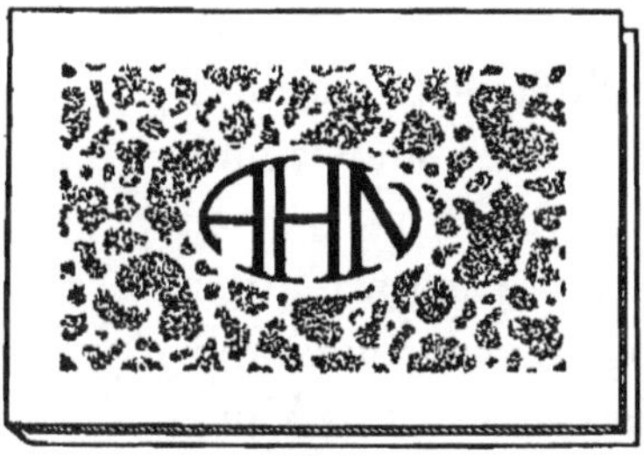
AHN
No 2

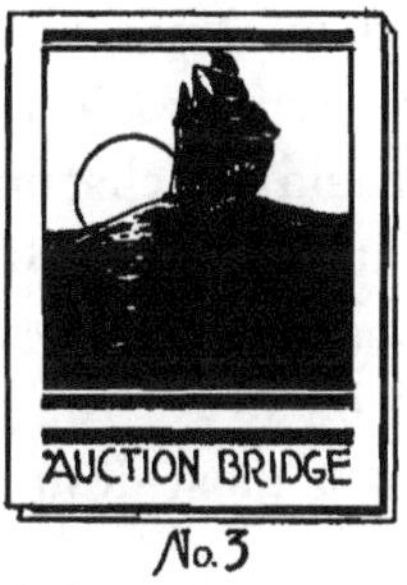
AUCTION BRIDGE
No.3

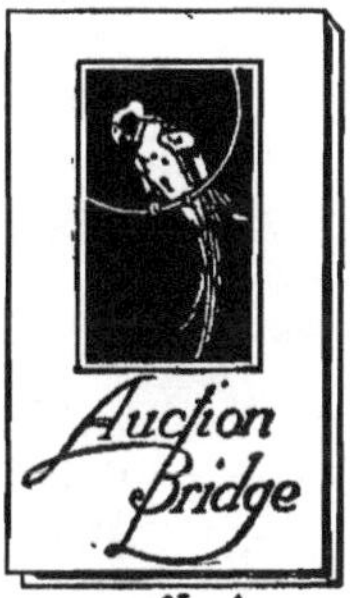
Auction Bridge
No.4

PLATE No. 13

# Birth Announcements and Congratulations

Birth announcements to be of real interest should be treated with a subtle touch of humor. They should be small in size and dainty in color and execution. In other words, they should be cute. The more formal engraved type is acceptable and very often used, but as in our discussion of other cards, we would stress the point of individuality. Certainly no other occasion gives greater inspiration for originality. You have in this case the rather difficult problem of giving out statistics in an attractive way, so you must remember that the wording of your message is the important item and your design or illustration should merely decorate this.

### Analysis of Plate No. 14

No. 1 illustrates a formal type of card and in the original was printed in gold on a delicately tinted card.

No. 2 and No. 3 have the desirable touch of delicate humor and the illustration admirably supplements the verses.

No. 4 is a bit more formal in character but avoids stiffness by its illustrations.

No. 5 is more informal and intimate and gives the desired information humorously yet fully. A card of this type would not be difficult to execute.

No. 6 could be charmingly colored and would be a delightful welcome for any baby.

No. 7 and No. 8 show attractive congratulation cards and illustrate the feeling of daintiness and charm that is most desirable in cards of this kind.

No. 1

BORN

No. 2

Sugar an' spice an' everything nice
that's what _____'s made of—

The day          The proud parents

No. 3

Engines an' sails, baseballs an' nails
that's what _____'s made of—

The proud parents

The day

No. 4

Just arrived at our

THE DATE
NAME
THE PROUD PARENTS

No. 6

Welcome little stranger

No. 5

Hip Hip Hooray!
HIS NAME IS JOHN
JULY TENTH WAS THE DAY
MARY AND JOHN JONES

No. 7

Congratulations
I'm sending dear BABY
My love and good wishes
And the best of regards
To the MR and MRS.

No. 8

My Love To Baby
Here's a loving welcome
to BABY WEE
And a great big wish
from GROWN UP ME.

PLATE No. 14

# Every Day Greetings

THERE are so many other occasions on which greeting cards are desirable that we cannot hope to find space for them all and so have grouped in two plates a few of the most important ones. We have chosen examples adaptable to different cards of the same class. An every day greeting is really a decorated sentiment, and whatever the occasion you wish to celebrate you will find that the thought behind the card is what will govern its design. The decorative effect of cards of this type depends as much upon the lettering as it does upon the motif. For example, the same flower motif could appropriately illustrate a greeting to a friend back from a trip or to a shut-in acquaintance. The effectiveness of each card would depend entirely upon how you expressed the welcome you wished to convey or the sympathy you wished to express and on the design and spacing of your lettering. One card might be awkward and stilted in feeling, regardless of the charm of the design used on the card, while the other one would be spontaneous and sincere and would convey to its recipient the exact feeling you had in designing it. So be sure your words are right then go ahead and decorate them as attractively as you wish.

Certain every day cards are informal and lend themselves to humorous treatment but there is a certain type that must be kept severely simple in design and must have the most carefully designed and executed lettering. Cards of condolence and Mothers Day cards both come under this last heading and depend for their sincerity upon their simplicity and good taste. In designing these cards it is well to keep in mind that the decoration must of necessity be so restrained that the texture and tint of the paper can add much and will be much more noticeable than in a more decorated card. If you decide to use a double card you can separate your decoration and sentiment and give yourself more chance for design and color in your motif on the cover, while the sentiment inside the card can be more elaborately designed also.

## Analysis of Plate No. 15

No. 1 and No. 4 illustrate the simplicity and restraint necessary for this type of card. The greetings are expressive and carry the whole feeling of the card, while the carefully designed lettering forms the real decoration.

No. 2 gives a chance for humor which has been amusingly illustrated. It would be permissible to use a more formal illustration on this card, though, without spoiling the thought you have expressed in your sentiment.

No. 3 is again illustrative of the necessity for attractive lettering and simplicity of design.

No. 5 illustrates a double fold card where there is more opportunity for design and illustration.

Delicate colors and dainty ribbons are necessary for this type of card.

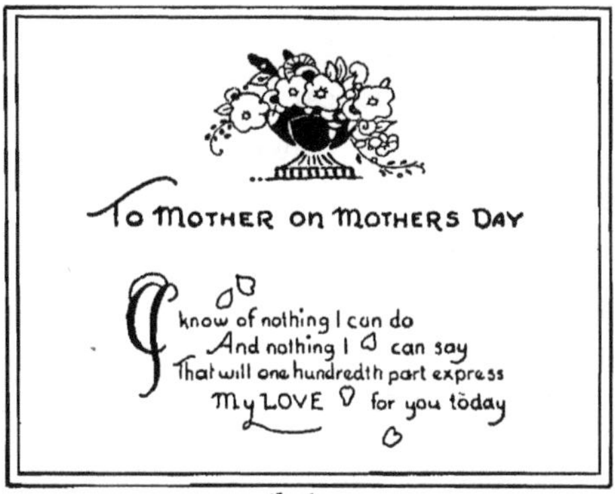
To Mother on Mothers Day
I know of nothing I can do
And nothing I can say
That will one hundredth part express
My LOVE for you today

No.1

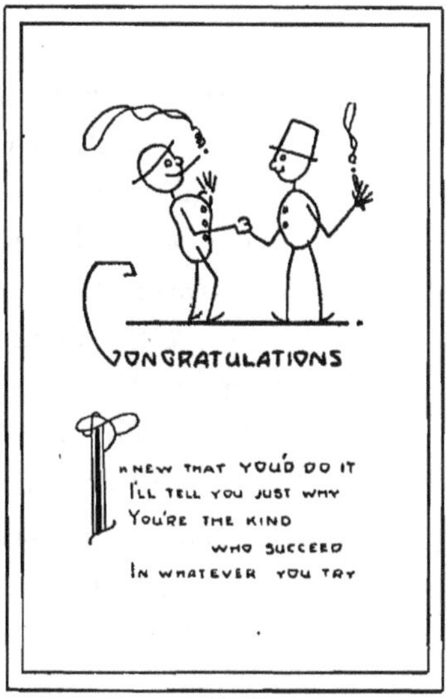
CONGRATULATIONS
I KNEW THAT YOU'D DO IT
I'LL TELL YOU JUST WHY
YOU'RE THE KIND
WHO SUCCEED
IN WHATEVER YOU TRY

No. 2

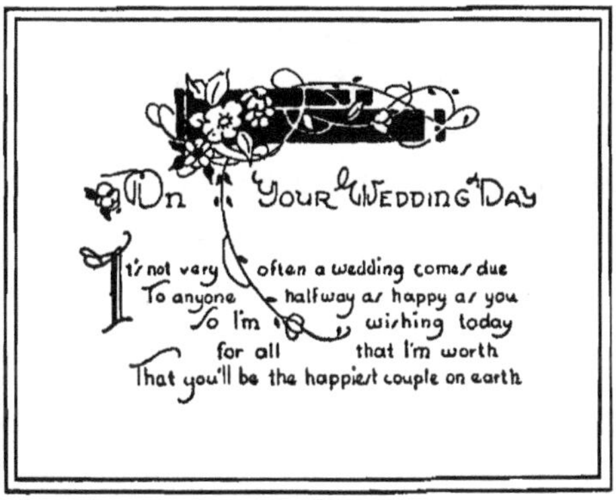
On Your Wedding Day
It's not very often a wedding comes due
To anyone halfway as happy as you
So I'm wishing today
for all that I'm worth
That you'll be the happiest couple on earth

No 3

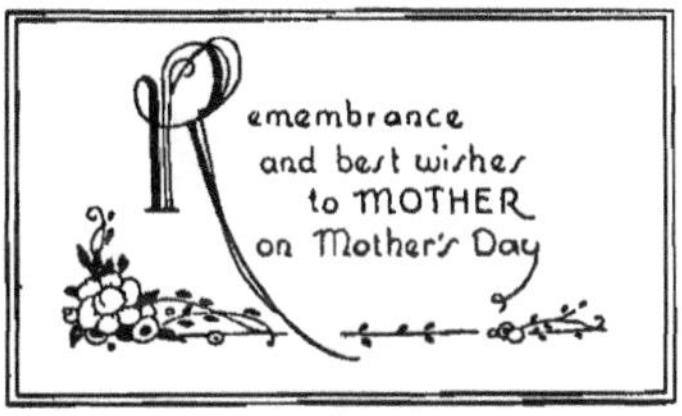
Remembrance
and best wishes
to MOTHER
on Mother's Day

No. 4

No 5

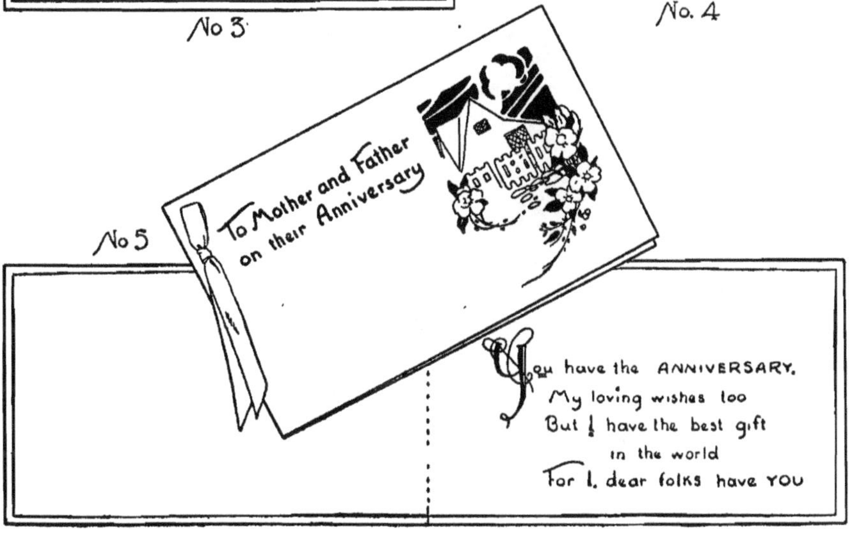
To Mother and Father
on their Anniversary
You have the ANNIVERSARY,
My loving wishes too
But I have the best gift
in the world
For I, dear folks have YOU

Plate No. 15

## Analysis of Plate No. 16

No. 1 is a delightful *Bon Voyage* card that is modern in design and original in sentiment. The original of this card was printed in black on a gray paper with the one touch of color the red of the smokestacks.

No. 2 shows an idea that can be amusingly depicted in both verse and illustration.

No. 3, No. 5 and No. 7 all emphasize the necessity for design in lettering and simplicity in composition as discussed above.

No. 4 shows the same necessity to an even greater degree. The original of this card was printed in a soft gray on a gray paper and was restrained in feeling and subdued in color.

No. 6 illustrates how a simple illustration can supplement the text of your message pleasingly but not obtrusively.

**No 1**

—only seasickness (and money) prevent me from going with you— Bon Voyage —

**No. 2**

missing you

I am so doggone lonesome
I feel so doggone blue
There's just one thing will comfort me,
That thing is seeing you

**No. 3**

Friends Like You

It's friendship makes the world go round
It's friendship makes it smile ooo
I know because it's friends like YOU
Make living worth the while

**No. 4**

WITH HEARTFELT SYMPATHY

Words cannot in the smallest part convey
The sympathy I have for you today
The wish I could in some small measure share
The poignant sorrow that is yours to bear

**No 5**

MY BEST TO YOU OLD FRIEND

**No 6**

TO A SHUT IN FRIEND

It isn't the easiest thing in the world
To smile when the clouds are gray
But I hope that you'll find
That they're all silver lined
On even the cloudiest day

**No. 7**

Forget You Not

A wee little blossom
I'm sending to you
With a heart full of gold
and with petals of blue
Forget me not

PLATE No. 16

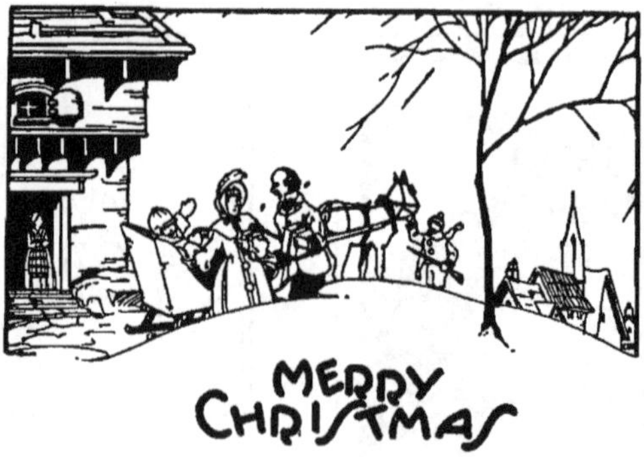
MERRY
CHRISTMAS

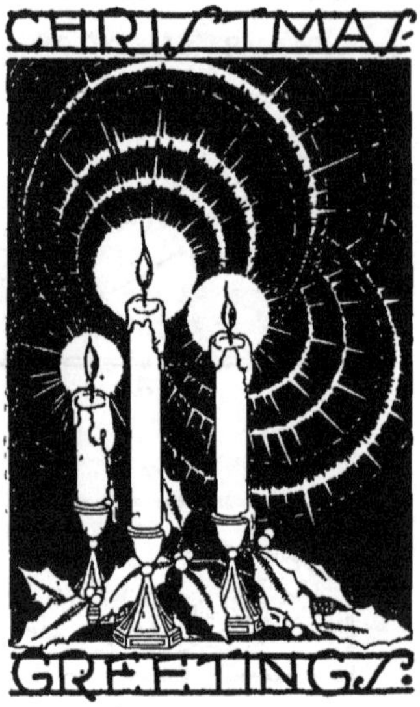
CHRISTMAS
GREETINGS

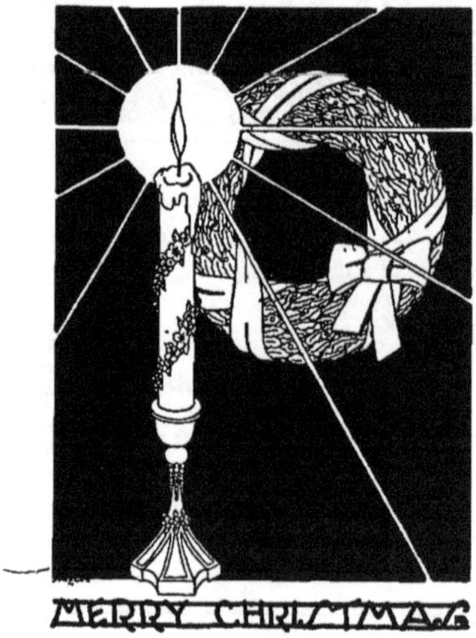
MERRY CHRISTMAS

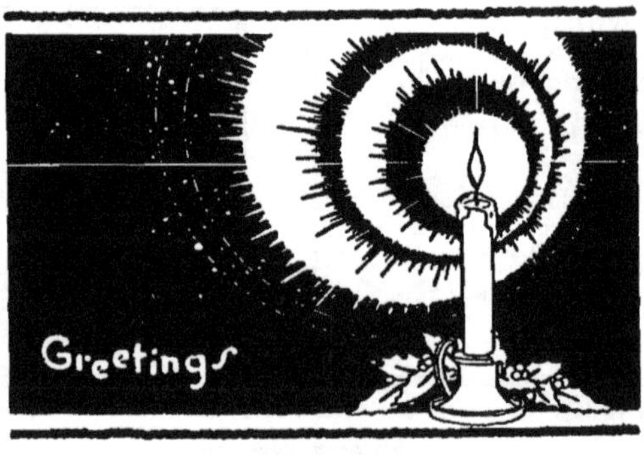
Greetings

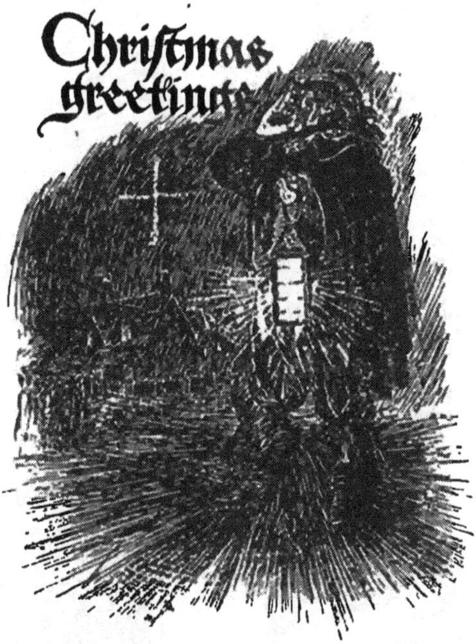
Christmas
greetings

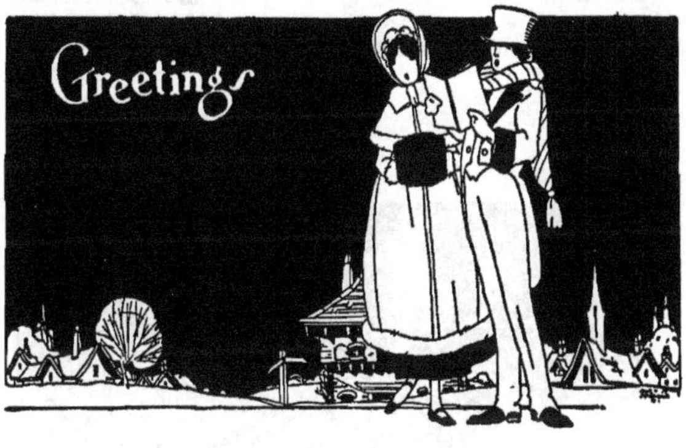
Greetings

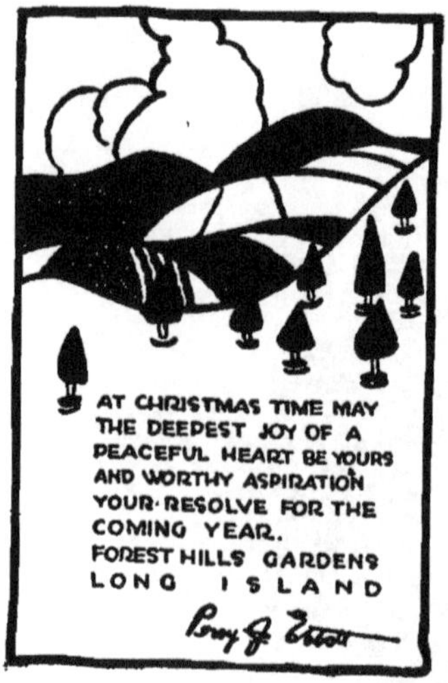


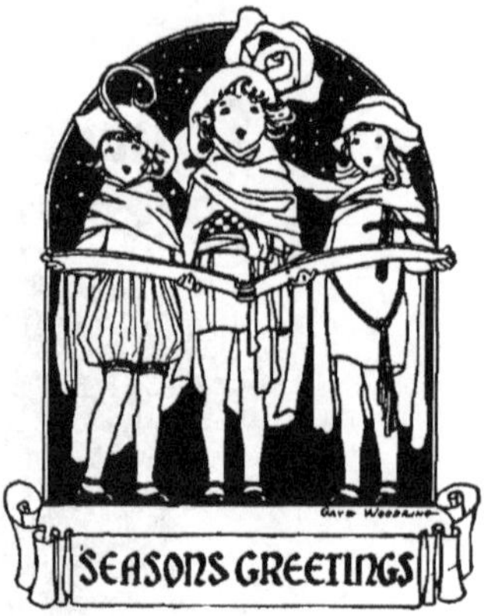


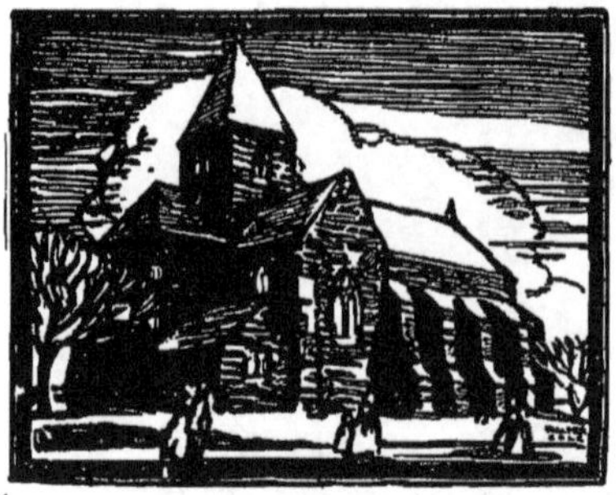

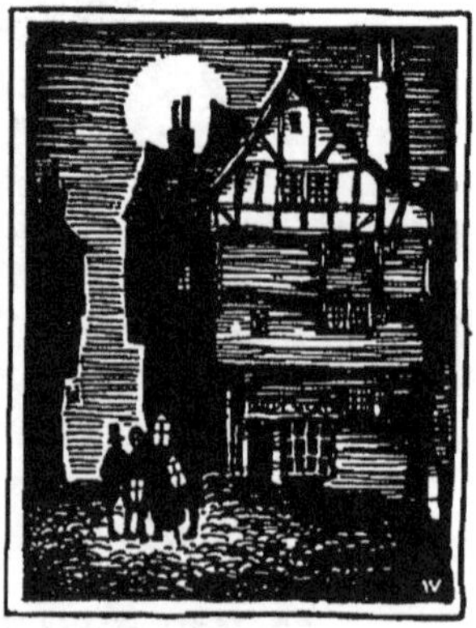

NOEL·NOEL·NOEL

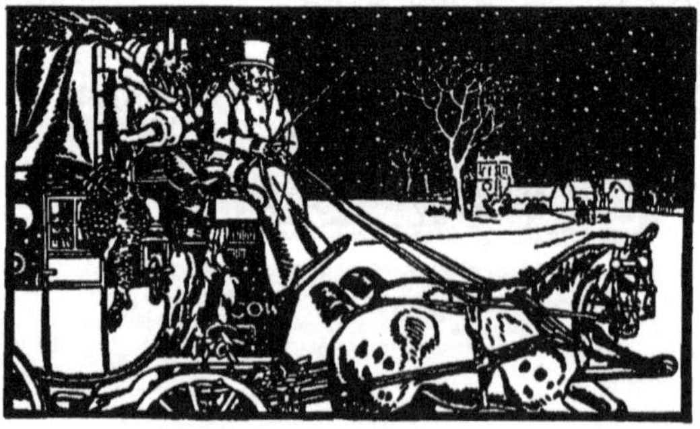

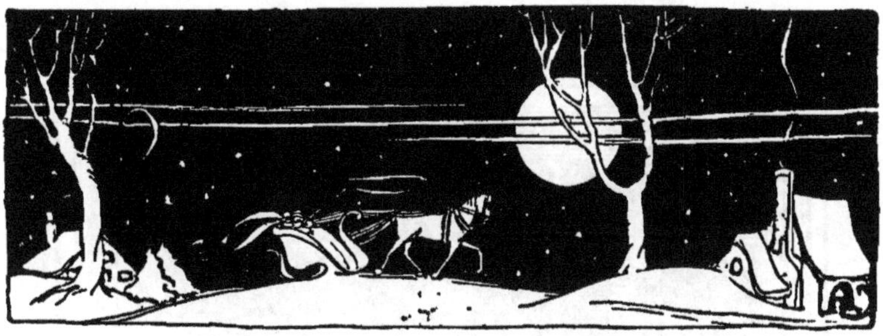

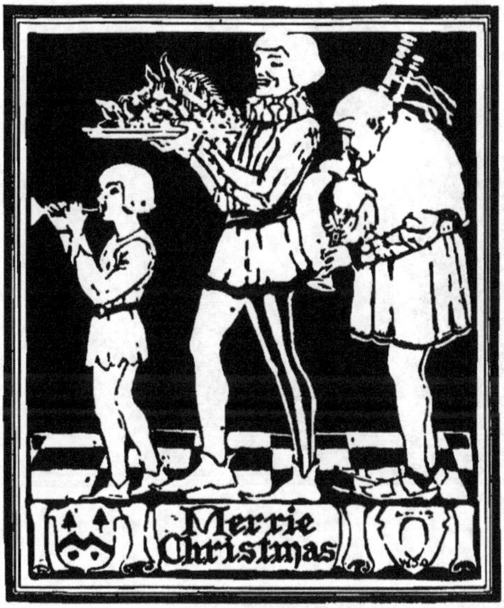
Merrie
Christmas

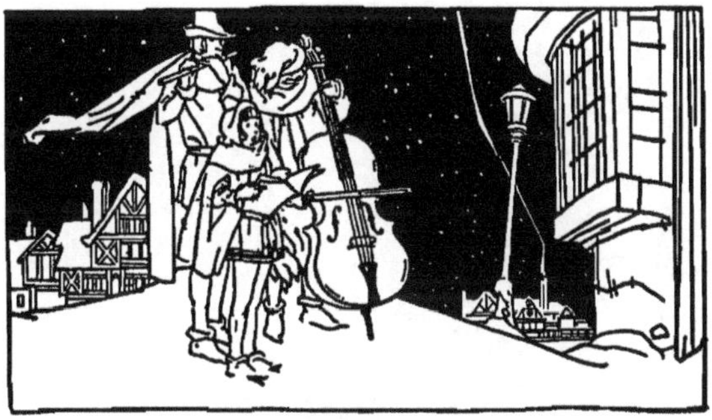

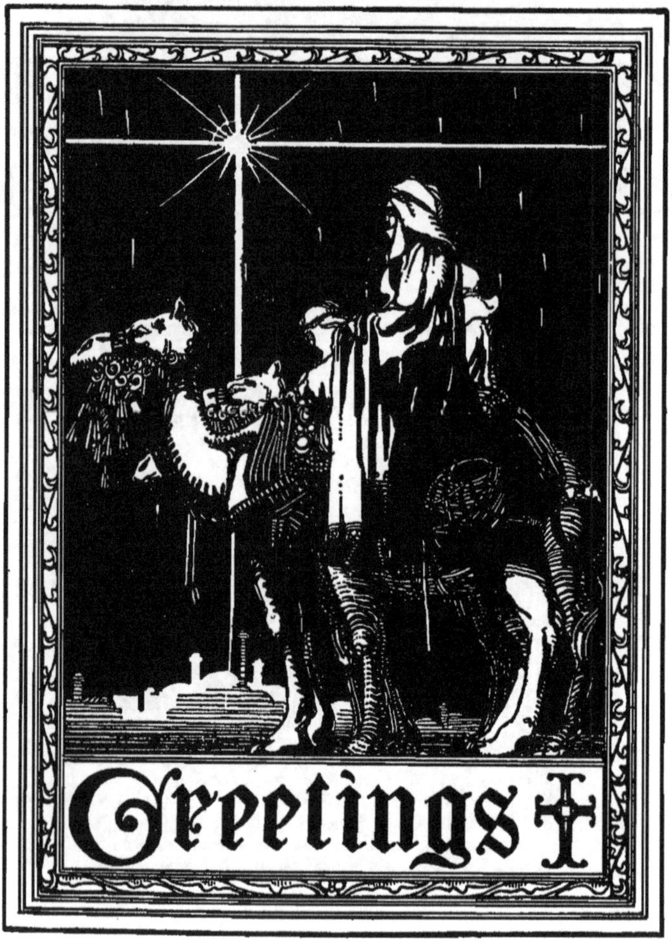
Greetings

# Things to Remember

THAT in designing a greeting card the idea or motif is the most important thing.

That a distinctive paper and unusual fold will greatly enhance your design.

That it is easier to work out the best possible composition by making several rough sketches to arrive at the best arrangement.

That you should have plenty of margin around your design.

That the lettering should be in harmony with the motif, should be well designed and carefully executed and should be at all times considered as an important part of the composition.

That the sentiment, motif and lettering should harmonize.

That you can secure from the publishers of this book uncolored cards for hand-coloring.

That you can secure our cooperation in the presentation of suitable ideas or drawings for publication either by us as Greeting Card Manufacturers or we will advise you with whom to communicate.

That we have attempted to show you by the text and the plates in this booklet how to design cards for any occasion and, though we could not possibly touch upon the numerous ones that might come to you, we hope that our suggestions and illusrations will be of real value.

That we would like to emphasize several points made in the above text and beg you to keep them in mind.

That, after several efforts toward perfection in the various phases of greeting card designing you will find that your ideas are prolific and your execution of them suitable and that it will be possible for you to market some of the most original ones with us as publishers of greeting cards.

That in no field of art is there more chance for originality of expression. Novel ideas can demand money.

That you will, at any rate we are sure, find the work delightful and engrossing and will get much pleasure, we hope, from your efforts in the many directions we have suggested.

www.ingramcontent.com/pod-product-compliance
Lightning Source LLC
Chambersburg PA
CBHW052200240425
25704CB00003B/13
* 9 7 8 1 2 5 8 4 5 5 7 2 9 *